# NANTUCKET
## in the
## Ninteenth Century

12/25/79

Dear Mom & Dad —
Hope you enjoy your journey
into the past through this book.

Love
Anne & Tom

# NANTUCKET
## in the
## Ninteenth Century

180 Photographs and Illustrations

by

CLAY LANCASTER

DOVER PUBLICATIONS, INC.
NEW YORK

To the Esteemed Librarians of the
Nantucket Atheneum

BARBARA P. ANDREWS
and
JANICE L. WILLIAMS

This Book is
Appreciatively Dedicated

---

*Frontispiece.* The Old Pump, Orange Street at Beaver Lane,
late 1860s (see Plate 69).

Published in Canada by General Publishing Company,
Ltd., 30 Lesmill Road, Don Mills, Toronto, Ontario.
Published in the United Kingdom by Constable and
Company, Ltd., 10 Orange Street, London WC2H 7EG.

*Nantucket in the Nineteenth Century: 180 Photographs and
Illustrations* is a new work, first published by Dover Publications,
Inc., in 1979.

*Book design by Carol Belanger Grafton*

*International Standard Book Number: 0-486-23747-8*
*Library of Congress Catalog Card Number: 77-75512*

Manufactured in the United States of America
Dover Publications, Inc.
180 Varick Street
New York, N.Y. 10014

# Contents

# List of Illustrations

(Credits are provided in each caption. Photographs and drawings not otherwise dated or credited are by the author.)

## VIEWS FROM TWO TOWERS

## STREET SCENES AND BUILDINGS IN NANTUCKET TOWN

## TRANSPORTATION

## THE GREAT HOTELS

## RECREATION CENTERS

## INTERESTING PEOPLE AND EVENTS AT THE END OF THE CENTURY

# Introduction

## THE ISLAND AND ITS EARLY SETTLERS

Nantucket rises from the Atlantic Ocean like a misshapen crescent moon (Figure A). It is embraced by water, and it embraces water, with Madaket Harbor at the west end and the Great Harbor in the deep cusp provided by Coatue at the northeast. Reaching upward is the narrow peninsula ending at Great Point, imitating in miniature the gesture of the forearm and elbow of Cape Cod, minus the fist, twenty to fifty miles due north. The long stretch of the south shore of Nantucket measures about thirteen or fourteen miles from Siasconset west to Great Neck. A ridge bisects the main body of the island, the highest point about ninety feet above sea level. The ridge was created in the Quarternary Period by glaciers and indicates the extent of their progress. Promontories distinguish the east shore of Nantucket, and Tom Nevers Head is below the curve (lower right-hand corner, Figure A). Quanaty Bank rises at the west end of the Great Harbor, and North Cliff, near Town, overlooks the Sound. Elsewhere the terrain slopes down to the sea, with numerous freshwater ponds approaching the perimeter. The largest are Long Pond near Madaket ("Maddequet" in Figure A), Hummock and Miacomet ponds at the south, Sachacha Pond on the east side and Coskata Pond above the Head of the Harbor. Waves lapping or hurling themselves upon the beach provide a changing, pulsating outline to the island.

The island was called Nantucket, the "Far-away Land," by the Indians. Ancient races had inhabited Nantucket when it was connected with the mainland and during the five thousand years of its isolation in the sea, other groups preceded the Indians living here when the white man came. The Indian must have eked a meager existence from the sandy soil on the island, with its limited vegetation, where there were no great trees to provide bark for shelters and where the largest animals were deer and seals, the last dwelling on the smaller islands (especially Muskeget; Figure A, left) to the west. Pelts must have been precious for clothing, and grass mats must have been woven to keep out the weather. The Indians turned to the water to supplement the limited supplies provided by the land. They sought shellfish, and they engaged in offshore fishing and even whaling (the last only of the smaller species). When the sea cast up larger specimens, the Indians would appropriate anything useful from the carcasses. The resourcefulness and thrift of the Indians offered a practical lesson to the English who followed.

The fact that King Charles I of England conveyed certain islands off the American coast—from Maine (Pemaquid) to Connecticut (Long Island)—to William, Earl of Sterling in 1635 had little effect upon Nantucket (which was included), until the Earl's agent sold it to Thomas Mayhew and Thomas Mayhew II in 1641. The two Mayhews shortly thereafter bought and settled on nearby Martha's Vineyard, and their early activity on Nantucket was limited to Christianizing the Indians. The fortunes of the island took a new direction when Tristram Coffin and others of Salisbury, determined to escape the religious bigotry and persecution that had followed the Pilgrim escapees even to the New World, sought to establish themselves and their families on some island south of the Massachusetts Bay Colony. In 1659 Tristram Coffin, Edward Starbuck and Isaac Coleman (a twelve-year-old orphan) visited Martha's Vineyard. Learning that Thomas Mayhew was willing to dispose of most of Nantucket, they traveled there to consider the island's suitability for their purpose. The outcome of the visit was that nine of the men from Salisbury each took a partner and with the two Mayhews formed a proprietary to purchase and settle Nantucket. For the western end of the island Mayhew was paid thirty pounds and two beaver hats (besides his own one-twentieth share), and later an additional five pounds for Tuckernuck Island, with the understanding that additional land was to be purchased from the Indians. In the fall of 1659 Thomas Macy, his wife and five children, Edward Starbuck, James Coffin and Isaac Coleman settled on Nantucket. They found the Indians kind and hospitable and spent the winter in a little hut at Madaket. Their Indian hosts little realized that within a short

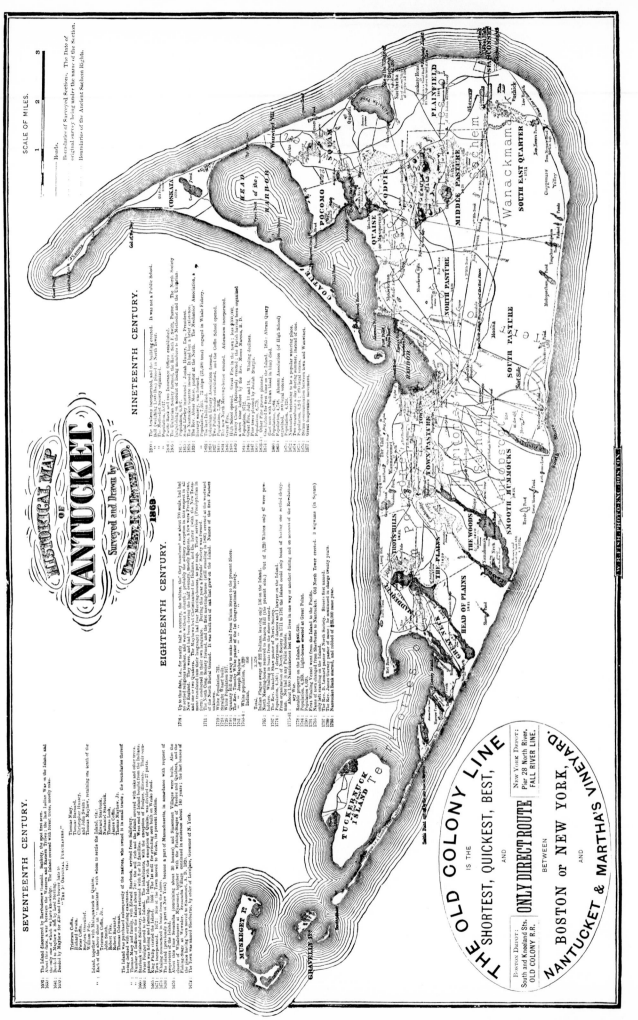

*Figure A.* Historical Map of Nantucket. Surveyed and Drawn by the Rev. F. C. Ewer, D. D. 1869 (Old Colony R. R. Reprint, ca. 1877, Library of Congress Collection).

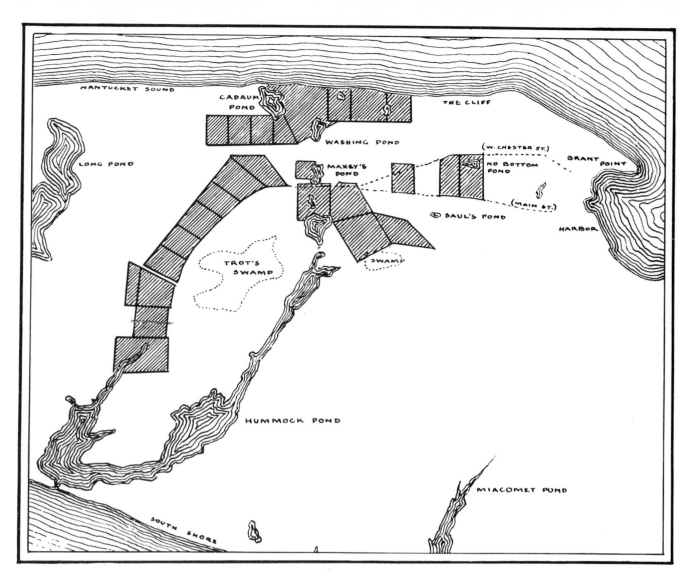

*Figure B.* Diagram Showing the Original Home Sites (shaded by diagonal lines) of the Late Seventeenth Century.

while the newcomers would own the entire island, that within a hundred years plagues would wipe out all but a fraction of their race, and that by 1855 their tribe would be extinct.

## ESTABLISHING THE ENGLISH COMMUNITY

For the most part the family names of the original English proprietors or First Purchasers were to reappear throughout Nantucket history. Besides Tristram Coffin, his son James, Thomas Macy, Edward Starbuck and the Mayhews, there were Tristram's other sons Peter and Tristram II, his sons-in-law Stephen Greenleaf and Nathaniel Starbuck, and Thomas and Robert Barnard, Thomas Coleman, Christopher Hussey, Thomas Look, William Pile, Robert Pike, John Smith, and John and Richard Swain—twenty

in all. In the spring of 1660 Edward Starbuck returned to the mainland and brought mechanics to the island to help with construction. Each was offered a half-share in the proprietary, and as the half-share membership rose to fourteen, the total number of shares became twenty-seven. Nantucket soil was poor for farming, but as it was suitable for raising sheep the early island industry was the production of wool. Most of the land was turned into sheep commons, with the animals (identified as to private ownership) allowed to roam free. A ditch was dug to keep them off the Indians' holdings, and in 1661 when the proprietors chose homesites, these were enclosed by fences. A homesite of sixty square rods was allotted to each whole share.

The settlement was incorporated under the name of Nantucket in 1671, the year the island became part of New York Province. Two years later Royal Governor Francis Lovelace renamed the settlement

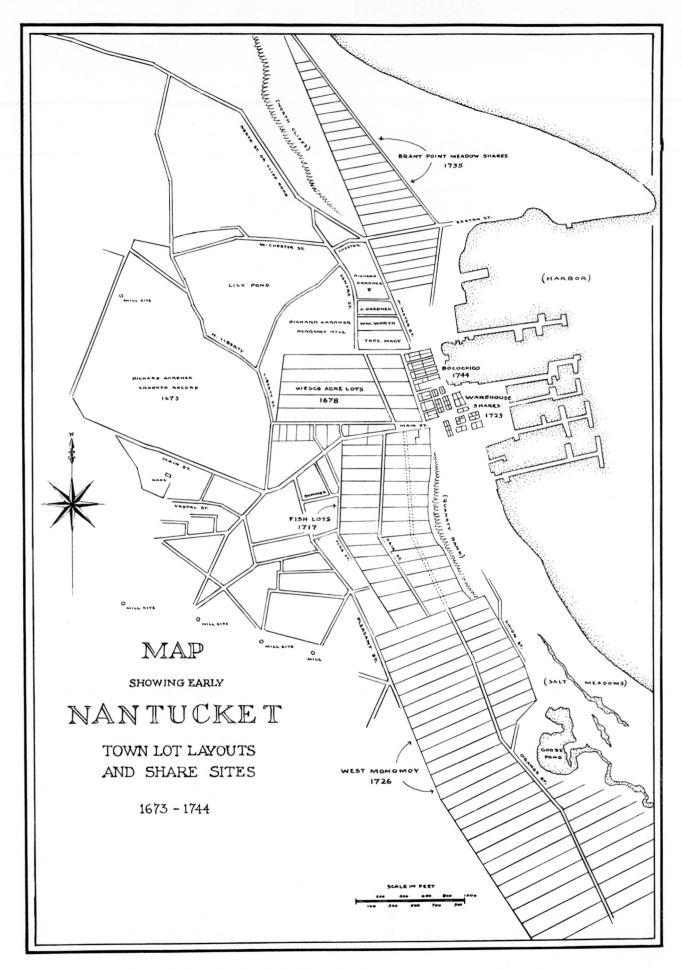

MAP

SHOWING EARLY

NANTUCKET

TOWN LOT LAYOUTS
AND SHARE SITES

1673 - 1744

*Figure* C. Map Showing Early Nantucket Town Lot Layouts and Share Sites,
1673–1744.

Sherborn (more often rendered "Sherburne") at the request of John and Richard Gardner (two half-share men) who wished to memorialize their ancestral village in England. But the newer designation caused trouble after 1692, when Nantucket became part of Massachusetts, as this province already contained a community of the same name. The two places endured the inconvenience of having identical names for more than a century, until the island town reverted to its original name in 1795. Since then "Nantucket" has denoted the island, the county and the town.

The original homesites formed what later generations would call a gerrymander shape from Capaum Pond (which had been the settlers' harbor until a storm raised a sandbar closing it from the Sound early in the eighteenth century) down to the west fork of Hummock Pond, and from the north portion east to the Great Harbor (Figure B). There was no semblance of a village, as each house presided over its own domain, each facing south to take advantage of solar heat through front windows in the winter. The common house-type consisted of a single room on each of two floors and a "porch" or entry with winder stairs connecting the two levels (Plate 61A). Referred to as an "English" house, it was much like the kind William Penn recommended to seventeenth-century immigrants to Pennsylvania. On occasion the early Nantucket house became double, with rooms on both sides of the chimney and stair-entry, as in the Jethro Coffin house (Plates 6 and 6A). The walls of this building were less than two full stories, although there were three floor levels in the residence. This type of structure was to become prevalent on the island, where few story-and-a-half Cape Cod cottages were built. Timbers for the Coffin house came from Exeter, N.H., where Jethro's father, Peter (son of the founder Tristram), had become the owner of large woodlands and a sawmill. These holdings proved to be quite lucrative: since Nantucket was without trees of sufficient size for house framing, Peter Coffin had a ready market for his lumber. Windows were imported and contained leaded lozenge panes in wood casements.

As with the Jethro Coffin house, which is on Sunset Hill, later homesites entered the limits of Nantucket Town. The first regularly plotted lot shares were established here in 1678. The region was called Wesco (the Indian word for white rock, and used to describe the area where a quartz was discovered on the site of the later Straight Wharf), extending from Quanaty Bank (Wesco Hill) to Lily Pond (Wesco Pond), and the shares were referred to as the Wesco Acre Lots. They reached from Broad Street to Liberty Street, and from Federal Street to the present Westminster Street, and contained five "squadrons" or horizontal rectangles cut by Centre Street (running at an angle up from Main Street, Figure C). Thomas Macy's homesite above Broad Street and Richard Gardner's to the north and west were both the easternmost and latest of the original homesites, and they were considered part of the Wesco Acre division. Early in the eighteenth century the Wesco Acre Lots were divided further. Though building sites became small, houses continued to be built facing south, thus sometimes putting their back sides on the public way (Plate 80).

By the beginning of the eighteenth century the type of residence had changed from the English to the lean-to (saltbox) house. The Nathan Coffin house (Plate 80), an example of the latter, differed from the earlier English version in having a one-story extension at the rear, covered by a long roof slope, and sash windows with wood muntins instead of leaded casements. The main distinction inside was the separation of the two functions of the former great room; the first floor now contained a parlor and distinct kitchen (with an oven in its fireplace) at the back (Plate 80A). A tiny "borning room" (the room in which women gave birth) and pantry with scuttle to the round cellar were also included. The Elihu Coleman house, the last built on the earliest division west of town, is an example of a double lean-to (Plate 7).

The lean-to type prevailed in the next subdivision in town, the Fish Lots Shares of 1717. Here and from this time onward the number of lots was set at twenty-seven. The Fish Lots were arranged to either side of Fair Street, and extended to Quanaty Bank on the east and to Pine Street on the west. The Thomas Macy house was one of the earliest built, or possibly moved here (Plate 63, left edge). It would seem that most of the old houses in the western location were transported and set up on the new town sites, as in the case of Parliament House (Plate 61). The George Bunker house was built on the Fish Lots originally as a lean-to; later its form was altered to accommodate an addition (Plate 64).

Two large subdivisions were laid out in 1726, each containing the prescribed twenty-seven sections. One of them, South Monomoy, was below the harbor and was not developed. The other, West Monomoy, adjacent to the Fish Lots, was settled slowly at first, with little new construction, but a century later the northern half was fairly well populated. The Isaiah Nicholson house in share No. 10, built in 1833, is probably the last of the island's lean-tos (Plate 70). Orange Street, which bisects the West Monomoy lots, was extended through the east range of the Fish Lots to Main Street. About this time Union Street was cut below Quanaty Bank, and a series of cross streets were laid through the west range of the Fish Lots, one to each share (Figure D, below center, right). The new streets, dating from the second quarter of the eighteenth century, diminished the size of the lots

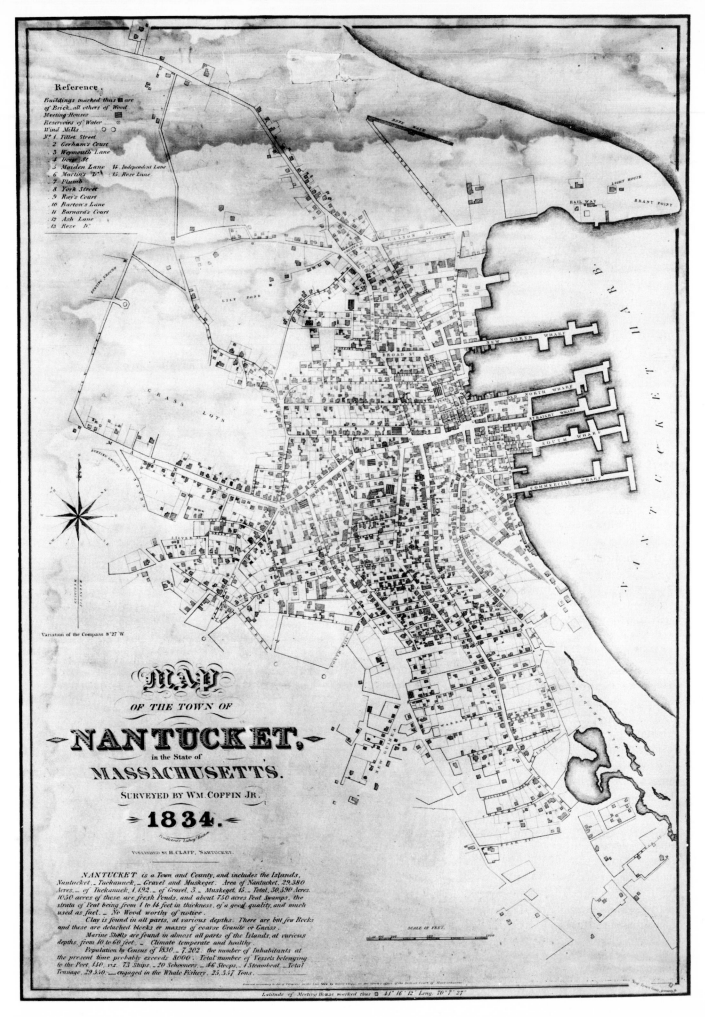

*Figure D.* Map of the Town of Nantucket . . . Surveyed by Wm. Coffin Jr. 1834
(New York Public Library Collection).

and prompted builders to face houses toward the street rather than the south. For the first time Nantucket took on the aspect of an orthodox town.

The next group of lots to be surveyed was the Brant Point Meadow Shares of 1735. The west boundary was North Water Street and a continuation of its line north of Easton Street, with Beach Street on the east. Only those shares adjoining and south of Easton Street were developed. Some of these were for commercial purposes, such as the ropewalk shown at the top of the William Coffin map of 1834 (Figure D).

The first wharf in the Great Harbor was built during 1716 or the following year, and in 1723 Richard Macy constructed the original Straight Wharf. The piers symbolized the new island vocations, shipping and whaling, which soon overshadowed sheep raising. The locale around the waterfront was undesirable for homes but acquired a commmerical value. The Warehouse Shares, surrounding the head of Straight Wharf, were divided in 1723. To the east of Wesco Acre Lots, Bocochico (perhaps derived from the Spanish for "small streams") was portioned in 1744. Lots were considerably smaller than heretofore, as they were intended for contiguous business buildings. The new type of structure fostered here was the gambrel-roofed warehouse, such as the three examples on the Square at the foot of Main Street (Plates 21 and 45A). However, noncommercial buildings went up in Bocochico, including residences and the Universalist Church, later the Atheneum (Plate 25). In 1765 the Beach Shares were laid out in the vicinity of South Wharf and Commercial Wharf, mostly below the Warehouse Shares. The Wharf Lots were staked off around Old North Wharf in 1770, expanding up to New North (later Steamboat) Wharf in 1774. In 1805 the South Beach Shares were added to the Beach Shares of 1765, and a North Beach division was surveyed at the base of Brant Point, adjoining the Brant Point Meadow Shares below Easton Street.

During the eighteenth century and up to the mid-nineteenth century Nantucket Town spread beyond most of the proprietary layouts (with the exception of the Brant Point Meadow Shares at the north and the South Monomoy Shares at the south), and included certain smaller lots ranged along the south side of Liberty and Main Streets. The town also expanded into the area west of the Fish Lots (Plates 49–52) and into the two holdings of Richard Gardner, Crooked Record (Plates 53–55) and Academy Hill (Plates 77 and 85–88), and out along West Chester and North Streets (Plates 33 and 34). Other parts of the island were also partitioned among the proprietors during the eighteenth century, accounting for the village that existed at Sachacha around 1800 and the still flourishing community of Siasconset (Plates 100–110).

## THE SOCIETY OF FRIENDS

A major factor in island history and culture was Quakerism, or the tenets of the Society of Friends. The unjust treatment of Friends on the mainland (including hangings in Boston) had contributed to the climate of intolerance which the First Purchasers sought to escape. Although the particular religious preferences of the original Nantucket settlers is not entirely known, it was only natural that Quakers would soon come to share the benefits of the remote sanctuary afforded by Nantucket. Thus it was that the gatherings held in Parliament House when it was the Nathaniel Starbuck home at the old settlement of Sherburne included Friends meetings (the first meeting on the island having taken place in 1708). Mrs. Mary Starbuck, daughter of Tristram Coffin, was a strong protagonist for the cause. The first structure built specifically for a Friends meetinghouse dates from about 1710 and stood on the rise of ground near the north head of Hummock Pond, not far from the first location of Parliament House. The meetinghouse, originally accommodating about two hundred persons, was later enlarged, and in 1731 a much greater meetinghouse was begun on the site of the old Quaker cemetery at the west end of Main Street. By this time the community on the Great Harbor was firmly established. The new building could seat fifteen hundred persons. But it, too, had to be enlarged, for by 1762 there were twenty-three hundred Friends on Nantucket. The predominantly Quaker population had rigid scruples against taking human life, and kept the island neutral during the American Revolution and War of 1812.

Quakers devised a dwelling that became the most numerous of any type on the island, and of which about one hundred seventy-five specimens survive today. Following the regime of the lean-to, the Quaker house dominated the building scene from the last quarter of the eighteenth century through the first quarter of the nineteenth century. The latter house-type is full two-storied, front and back, with rooms clustered around a central chimney, and has an asymmetrical facade of four bays, some with windows of unequal widths. The form of the structure is dictated by its plan, consisting of a parlor, stair hall and closet at the front and a kitchen and a chamber in the rear of the first story (Plate 58A). Three bedrooms occupy the second floor. Late examples are raised off the ground with full basements, and dressed up outside by pilastered doorways, cornice-hooded windows and clapboarded fronts (Plates 71 and 79), which are at odds with the casualness originally intended. It seems incredible, considering the plainness of many early Quaker houses, that they could have been considered enviable home settings. The interiors of many, however, belied their simple exteriors. On old Pearl Street, for example, the luxurious contents of the many Quaker houses there reminded one 1811 observer of the life-styles of Eastern potentates and led him to proclaim the street "India Row" (see Plate 76). The one Quaker house in the group filled with old Nantucket furnishings today displays a remarkable collection of Far Eastern chests and lacquered pieces, carvings, paintings, ceramics and other decorative objects.

## THE DEVELOPMENT OF NANTUCKET

The fortunes of Nantucketers were now derived mainly from outfitting whale ships. There were ropewalks, duck factories, cooper and block shops, and even a marine railway on Brant Point where ships were built, so that most of the requirements were produced locally. Joseph Starbuck was considered the richest man in town when he died in 1861 and his business endeavors were concentrated in the marine field. The Three Bricks, built for his sons, were monuments to the industry (Plate 50). Paul West established the nucleus of his wealth through a few whaling expeditions to the Pacific Ocean, then settled down as an investor in a number of New England banks, insurance companies and railroads. On the whole, local industries outside of the oil traffic were not very long-lived. Two that enjoyed a measure of endurance were the silk mill of the 1830–40s (Plate 82) and the straw-hat factory of the 1850–60s (Plate 42). The latter was prompted by the recession that was beginning to appear in oil merchandising. The cranberry industry was started at this time, but escalated much later (Plate 16).

The wealth amassed from whaling was reflected in houses more ample than the Quaker type. Joseph Starbuck's own residence, built in 1809 on New Dollar Lane, had a two-chimney, center-stair-hall plan, which provided considerably better circulation and more rooms than the single-chimney lean-to or Quaker house. The Edward Cary house, of similar layout, illustrates its advantages (Plates 53 and 53A). The Thomas Macy house was originally a Quaker type that was enlarged and remodeled into a transverse-passage type (Plate 51). The next step was putting chimneys not in the middle but on outside walls, as in the Frederick Mitchell and Philip H. Folger houses (Plates 42 and 46). Built of brick, these residences set the precedent for later shipowners' homes on Main Street, including the Henry and Charles G. Coffin houses and the Three Bricks (Plates 48 and 50). The basic design for each of the three Starbuck sons' homes was expanded for the Jared Coffin mansion on Broad Street (Plate 83). One notes a refinement in all these houses not found in other places, such as the absence of basement windows toward the street, thus screening the domestic duties of the nether region from public gaze.

Simultaneous with or even preceding the evolutionary changes in residences was the architectural development of public buildings. A significant point was reached in the elegant Masonic Lodge Hall of 1802, whose facade was organized by a giant Ionic pilastrade and included arched windows and elaborate details (Plate 48A). The adjoining Nantucket Pacific Bank, built in 1818, is a pleasing example of the Federal style (Plate 47). The Second Congregational Meetinghouse facade, as enlarged by Perez Jenkins in 1830, is a provincialization of a sophisticated house of worship at the Hub (Plates 65 and 66). The Washington House acquired that most noble of architectural devices, the freestanding colossal portico, in 1832. The building unfortunately burned four years later (Plate 21). About this time a great tetrastyle portico was added to the former Universalist Church, by then become the Atheneum, which was symbolic of its conversion from religious to cultural purposes (Plate 25). The little Gothic Revival Trinity Church, remodeled from a simple Friends meetinghouse in 1839, was a gem of the Romantic period (Plate 26). The new Atheneum, replacing the old one destroyed by fire a decade after its conversion, stands at the apex of Nantucket's revival architecture (Plate 90).

The ostentation of some of these public buildings is found in only two private Nantucket homes, both designed by Frederick Brown Coleman, architect of the new Atheneum (Plate 49). The houses were commissioned by William Hadwen, and each has a two-storied portico like that of the Atheneum. Hadwen's own house, at the corner of Main and Pleasant Streets, is one of the largest in town, and the adjoining home of his niece, although considerably smaller, is the peer of all on Nantucket in the matter of fine architectural detailing (Plate 49A). It has been suggested that the elaborateness of these buildings was prompted by Hadwen's birthplace, Newport, but the house in the Rhode Island town that could best serve as the model for the Hadwen niece's house (the Capt. Augustus Littlefield residence, ca. 1840, on Pelham Street) falls far short of Colemans' masterpiece in refinement.

When the architectural evolution of upper Main Street reached its zenith, lower Main Street was wiped out by the Great Fire on the night of 13 July 1846. About three hundred buildings were obliterated in Nantucket's most concentrated area. The devastation extended from just short of Commercial Wharf over to Washington Street, up and west on Main Street to Orange Street, and from the north side of Main Street between Centre Street and the harbor up to Broad Street, over to North Water Street up to Sea Street, thence over to the base of Brant Point. Two lessons were learned from the conflagration: the importance of having streets wide enough so flames could no leap across, and the necessity of using fireproof building materials. Thus the north side of Main Street was pushed back from the Square at the east end on a line with Liberty Street, and the cross streets—Centre, Federal and South Water—were increased in breadth. Buildings on the upper side of Main were rebuilt mostly of brick, with brownstone trim and slate roofs. They were formalized by pilasters and entablatures, and crowned by pediments (Plate 43). Except at the corner of Orange Street, buildings on the south side of Main remained low, and were executed shoddily in wood, with paint applied to give them the appearance of more permanent materials (Plate 44). During the early 1850s the upper and lower parts of Main Street were linked by the planting of American elm trees, the gift of Henry and Charles G. Coffin, whose homes benefited from the new street ornaments. Nantucket's retail businesses were now well-housed and shaded, but they did not prosper: the island never fully recovered from the disastrous fire of 1846.

The island's chief industry—producing whale oil—had been reduced to half by the introduction of camphine; it was cut another thirty percent by lard oil, and finally was given the deathblow by the production of kerosene from petroleum and by piped gas. Nantucket's own street lighting by gas began in 1854, when it was popular in the larger American communities. Already idled by the changing market, many Nantucket ships took prospectors to the California Gold Rush in 1849 and foundered in San Francisco Bay. The last whaler left Nantucket seeking sperm oil in 1869, but the ship never returned (Plate 19). It was the end of an era.

## NANTUCKET AS A SUMMER RESORT

In view of the depreciation of the whaling industry, it is remarkable that Nantucketers went to such pains and expense in filling the downtown gap as attractively as they did after the Great Fire of 1846. The breadth, unity and simple grandeur of the Greek Revival edifices erected in the commercial section gave focus to the town's architecture, a counterpart to the elegance of upper Main Street and a contrast to the quaintness elsewhere. Thus it was that when Nantucket's established economy failed, it still retained enough amenities in town and natural beauty elsewhere to cater properly to a new rewarding venture: tourism. During the middle of the nineteenth century vacationists turned from mountain watering places, with their mineral springs, to saltwater bathing in the Atlantic Ocean. Nantucket is surrounded entirely by a beach animated by surf, and its harbors have a shoreline caressed by gentle waters. Its pure and salubrious air blowing in from the sea keeps the island delightfully cool while the

mainland swelters. The old whaling port, providing a charming atmosphere, was gradually transformed into a place of ample guest accommodations to meet the growing demands.

Several of the plates in this book give some idea of what hostelries were like in Nantucket before the Great Fire of 1846. Little can be ascertained about the foremost, the Washington House, veiled behind surging flames and smoke in the Starbuck conflagration scene (Plate 21), except that it had a monumental portico, no doubt inspired by that of the Tremont House (1829) in Boston. Foreshortened views of the facades of the Mansion House on Federal Street are shown in the George G. Fish drawing (Plate 22), and of the Gardner House in the Main Street painting attributed to J. S. Hathaway (Plate 23). The obliteration of these buildings by fire made acute the need for a proper hotel in Nantucket. The island newspaper, the *Nantucket Inquirer*, singled out the ten-year-old Nantucket Steamboat Company as the proper agent to provide a suitable caravansary. The new three-story brick residence of Jared Coffin was standing empty, and the owner offered it to the Steamboat Company for $7,000, less than half the cost of its construction. The sale was completed, and on 14 May 1847 the Ocean House opened, and it has remained in operation with few interruptions from that time onward (Plate 83).

Small inns had dotted the island since the eighteenth century, but most of them were humble affairs, like Mother Cary's tavern (Plate 100). A major landmark in the hotel industry on Nantucket was the building of the Atlantic House in Siasconset, made available to the public a year after the Ocean House (Plate 103). Special carriages transported patrons from the steamboat to the village, and there, according to the *Nantucket Inquirer*, they could enjoy such recreational facilities as "Bowling, Bathing, Fishing and Fowling." The Atlantic House and the Ocean House dominated the scene until after the Civil War.

During the mid-1860s two long-lived Nantucket inns came into existence. One was Elijah Alley's Hotel on North Water Street (Plate 95), and the other was the Adams House, subsequently the Sherburne House, on Orange Street (Plate 67). The former became part of the nearby Springfield House complex (Plates 96 and 97), and the latter was sometimes operated in connection with neighboring institutions, such as the Bay View House (Plate 68). In the 1880s the Veranda House, on Step Lane (Plate 98), and The Nantucket, on Brant Point (Plate 118), entered the parade.

Except for the New Springfield (Plate 97), all of these inns were remodelings of older structures. Farther out from Town, however, there were no buildings suitable for conversion, and during the Reconstruction Era, when inns were erected in locales remote from Town, most were built from the ground up. The first of these was the Ocean View House at Siasconset. It was constructed by its owner-builder Charles H. Robinson in 1872–73, with a second pavilion dating from 1876 and a third from 1884 (Plates 105 and 106). Another new structure, the Wauwinet House, at the Head of the Harbor, was opened in 1876 and subsequently enlarged (Plate 125). The Surfside Hotel, however, was the rebuilding of an inn that had previously been located on the Providence River (Plate 114). The hostelry's regime at Nantucket's seaside dated from 1883. The railroad that had been built to Surfside two years earlier was also secondhand, and when its tracks were extended to Siasconset in 1884, the depot erected at the new terminus consisted of half of the Surfside station (the other half remained *in situ*) and was therefore a hand-me-down as well (Plates 112 and 115).

Summer cottages were no less important than hotels in sheltering seasonal visitors. The first advertisement for renting a cottage in the *Inquirer and Mirror* appeared in June 1865. The cottage was located on the North Cliff, which afforded lovely views of Nantucket Sound and the harbor, a fact which was mentioned in the sales pitch. Houses commissioned by perennial visitors began to be built in 1871, first on Main Street (Plate 42) and later in other parts of town. At Siasconset Charles H. Robinson built a summer cottage on Sunset Heights a year before the Ocean View House (Plate 104). Adjoining lots were offered for sale to persons desirous of constructing their own vacation domiciles. Later, E. F. Underhill made a thriving business in Siasconset by building new homes or buying and refurbishing existing cottages for summer occupancy (Plate 107). The success of renting houses led greedy entrepreneurs to purchase large tracts and divide them into lots arranged along street grids. Such "cottage cities" were laid out extensively beginning in the early 1870s, including a number ranging from the North Shore Hills out to Trots Hills and Wannacomet, and also the Sea Shore Enterprise below Madaket, Nauticon to the east, a few at the farther end of the Great Harbor, and some in Siasconset. The expected boom fizzled by the late 1870s, but the process was restarted in the 1880s, at Surfside, Sachacha, along Coatue, Brant Point and, once again, on the North Cliff.

The Sea Cliff Inn, opened in 1887, accompanied a revitalization of cottage building atop the Cliff in the same way The Nantucket had appeared as an outgrowth of the Brant Point subdivision three years earlier. The Sea Cliff Inn was the monarch of Nantucket hostelries. The building was designed and framed on the mainland especially for its site, and six years later its success justified a larger companion pavilion (Plates 120 and 121). For a hotel on

the island the Sea Cliff Inn had a unique location, commanding a promontory view, with a footpath to the water and within easy reach of Town yet not actually inside the community. The Point Breeze Hotel, which opened in 1891, emulated the Sea Cliff Inn—but more in its publicity than in its actual physical assets (Plate 122).

## VACATION ACTIVITIES

From the middle of the nineteenth century onward, all of the hostelries understood and catered to the summer visitors' penchant for sea bathing. Provisions for it were inaugurated by the Ocean House when taken over by Eben Allen in 1857 (Plates 27 and 123). In 1864 he erected a "Bathing House" on the Cliff Shore, but a long trek was necessary to reach these facilities. Five years later Charles E. Hayden designed and superintended the construction of the Clean Shore Bathing Rooms ("Clean Shore" being a preexisting name for this stretch) on the harbor north of Steamboat Wharf (Plate 35). In 1875 the first bathhouses appeared at Siasconset (Plates 109 and 110). During the nation's Centennial year, back in Town, Hayden added chambers containing tubs to the Clean Shore Rooms for hot saltwater soaking, and in 1880 he erected a second establishment beyond the jetties (near Allen's initial construction), called the Cliff Shore Bathhouses (Plate 123).

Another island diversion was the squantum, which was revived soon after the close of the Civil War. The term "squantum" is of Indian origin, and was used to describe a cruise by catboat with a collation at the destination, usually chowder or a clambake. They were held on the islets to the west or at various points about the Great Harbor. The Wauwinet House (1876) and the Cedar Beach House (1883) were outgrowths of the squantum movement (Plates 125 and 126). In their early days they were always reached by water.

Because of its location Nantucket's cuisine has traditionally specialized in seafood. In addition, from its inception as a vacation spa, ice cream has been a special summertime treat, and many ice-cream parlors have existed. As a seafaring place, with a prevalence of sailors, drinking was frowned upon, and the word "saloon" was applied to an ice-cream emporium and not to a bar. Many early saloons served both seafood and frozen desserts, and perhaps cakes and pies, but not strong drink. The ornamental soda fountain, resplendent with Italian marble and nickel-plated fixtures, was a phenomenon of the 1870s.

An annual event that began purely as a local activity was the County Fair, first held toward the end of October 1856, at the Atheneum. When the Nantucket Agricultural Society acquired its own fairgrounds in 1859 the gatherings were scheduled for earlier in the season. By the 1880s they were being given during the first week in September and after the advent of the new century in late August. The change of date was made to draw the summer traffic. Horse racing certainly was a concession to off-island patronage (Plate 124).

Performances of diverse types were popular summer entertainments. In June 1856 Spalding and Rogers' Great Railroad Circus, despite its name, arrived aboard the steamboat *Island Home* (Plate 32). Its tent show consisted mostly of equestrian acts punctuated by clown antics. In September 1857 the Peak family of "Vocalists, Harpers and Lancashire Bell Ringers" gave a boisterous performance in the upper hall of the Atheneum (Plate 90). During the following summer the local Dramatic Club presented a popular three-act comedy, *The Serious Family*, at the Atlantic House in Siasconset. Later in the century amateur theatricals were an important part of hotel life. The Nantucket had a small stage in its grand parlor (Plate 119), and the second pavilion of the Sea Cliff Inn had a basement theater (Plate 121). During the early 1900s, Siasconset became famous as an actors' summer colony. Musical numbers accompanied all major events, such as the inauguration of the Nantucket Railroad (Plate 111) and the Coffin family reunion at Surfside (Plate 113)—as well as elsewhere on the island. Orchestras for balls concluding a celebration were often derived from the ranks of concert bands that had provided music earlier. No social or patriotic function was considered of any consequence unless it terminated in a formal ball. These were held at the Surfside depot (Plate 112), at Atlantic Hall in Town (Plate 42) and at the various hotels. Both the Surfside depot and Atlantic Hall served as roller-skating rinks during the early 1880s, and when the latter was moved to Brant Point, a building was erected specifically for skating on Sea Street. Late in the century baseball games provided stimulation.

Nantucket loved to celebrate national holidays. It was at the George Washington Birthday party of 1832 that the name was chosen for Elisha Starbuck's hotel (Plate 21). A first-rate if impromptu festival was held on the completion of the laying of the Atlantic cable on 5 August 1858: the rejoicing proved premature, though, as the system ceased to operate shortly after the exchange of the initial messages. Pyrotechnics enlivened such affairs. The paramount summer patriotic fete was July 4th. Often it was marked by multiple events, as in 1873 when a social dance was proffered at the newly-opened Ocean View House at Siasconset in the afternoon, and a grand promenade and ball transpired at Atlantic Hall in town during the evening. In 1881 the inauguration of the Nantucket Railroad was scheduled on July 4th,

though its completion entailed working assiduously over a weekend. The extension of the tracks and opening of the Surfside Hotel at Nobadeer was celebrated on the same holiday two years later (Plate 114). The railroad was pushed on to Siasconset the next year, but due to work delays and inclement weather the target date was missed, and the completion exercises took place four days later on the "Glorious 8th" (Plate 115). Purposely scheduled a few days after the 4th was the momentous fin-de-siècle anniversary of shifting the town's name from Sherburne back to Nantucket and the two-hundredth anniversary of the county (Plate 130).

Tourists often paid visits to points of interest, historic places, topographical features, and happenings unique to the island. The Jethro Coffin house on Sunset Hill, an antiquity intimately connected with the early settlement, was already on the "must" list in the late nineteenth century (Plate 6). The last surviving windmill had become something of a curiosity even before its acquisition by the Nantucket Historical Association in 1897 (Plates 4 and 131). Lighthouses were exoticisms to most visitors (Plates 8 and 9), and so were the lifesaving stations which had given aid to distressed ships and their crews (Plate 11). If one happened to be on Nantucket when a wreck occurred (Plates 10 and 12), or when a large whale or school of small ones became stranded (Plate 18)—or on a day that combined a shipwreck and a whale (Plate 13)—the folks back home could expect a thrilling eyewitness account. Exploring the Great Harbor by catboat, crossing the moors by box cart, journeying to Siasconset by stagecoach or later by rail, and walking along the crest of the cliff from the old fishing village to Sankaty Head were popular pastimes. Summer-cottage residents sometimes amused themselves and added to their larder by picking huckleberries on the moors. During the regime of the Nantucket Railroad, passengers were let off with their empty buckets on the outgoing trip and taken aboard the train with ample supplies of berries on the return.

## NATIVE ECCENTRICS

Nantucket provided a steady supply of characters among its inhabitants, individuals whose acquaintance was as much part of the summer scene as Brant Point light. One was Capt. William Baxter, a former mariner who drove the Siasconset stagecoach (Plate 101). On a dark night, it was said, the captain would stop the coach, jab his whip into the road and lick a little of the dust off the end. When asked about this procedure Capt. Baxter would reply: "Why, bless you, I know this old island blindfolded. I just take a sounding and can tell to a foot where we are." Baxter

*Figure E.* A View of Siasconset a Fishing Village on Nantucket (Frontispiece to D. A. Leonard, *The Laws of Siasconset; A Ballad,* New Bedford, Mass., 1797, Nantucket Historical Association Collection).

also delivered the Siasconset mail and put a sign over the door of his house proclaiming it the "Post Office." Hearing of it, the postal authorities considered this illegal and sent an agent to investigate. The investigator boarded Baxter's stagecoach and, unaware of the driver's identity, told him of his mission. Baxter, swearing there was no such sign in Nantucket, made a left turn and drove him through nearby Polpis, proving the rumor totally false.

Even the famed Nantucket astronomer Maria Mitchell was something of a character (Plate 58). One story, related in *The Nantucket Scrap Basket* by William F. Macy and Roland B. Hussey (1916), states that after a doctor recommended she take lager beer as a tonic, she brought home a bottle. When her sister asked where she had got it, Miss Mitchell indicated the saloon on the corner. Her sister pointed out that no respectable woman ever entered such a place. Maria Mitchell was indignant over the inference. "Oh," she said, "I told the man he ought to be ashamed of his traffic!"

Elisha Pope Fearing Gardner lettered verses on placards and hung them on the fence of his home on Chicken Hill, which he called "Poet's Corner." Many people went to the kindly poet's domicile to read and ruminate. Gardner's sentiments were more nearly perfect than his meter, however.

Nantucket's best known eccentrics were those in the public employ, especially the town criers. These men were not elected nor put on the regular town payroll, though they were reimbursed for their services of keeping fire watch in South Tower and "calling" town affairs. Their pay was supplemented by announcing private sales and other events for a fee, and on the same basis they sometimes performed other odd jobs and sold newspapers. Charles H. Chase was a crier during the 1860s. According to *The Nantucket Scrap Basket*, one afternoon while he was on his rounds, ringing his bell to attract attention, a fresh summer miss asked him where he had got his bell. Chase flashed back: "Same place you got your manners, young woman—from the brass foundry!"

The town crier who became one of the most renowned persons on the island was William D. Clark (Plates 128 and 128A). Billy was invited to visit several cities on the mainland and was entertained as a celebrity. In 1885 he was given a place in the line of march with the local brass band and outfitted in a uniform. He carried the tin horn that was his instrument of office, which he normally blew to attract attention when announcing urgent matters from South Tower. Some thought his "musical" accompaniment no better than the braying of a donkey, but the *Inquirer and Mirror* looked beneficently on his new role in the band: "William is the most expert soloist in the organization." Another town crier, Alvin Hull, sometimes ran Clark a close

second in popularity and in other matters (Plate 129).

A public employee in a different capacity was Joseph Swain, janitor of the Atheneum and guide to its museum collection (Plate 91). Once when his tour group stood spellbound listening to his descriptions long after closing time and made no move to depart, Joe seized a wicked-looking implement from the shelf and swung it around his head: "This, ladies and gentlemen," he said, "is a genuine war club used by the savages of the Fiji Islands—I wish to God I was there!"

## ARTISTS OF EARLY NANTUCKET

A group of people with whom this book is very much concerned is that which provided illustrations of Nantucket. Very early picture records of the island are rare. The austerity of Quakerism precluded art. It was seen as a frivolity and vanity and therefore undesirably worldly. In this, the island attitude was not very different from that of most of New England, though elsewhere it was prompted by Puritanism. Nevertheless, the gaining of economic affluence was accompanied by a relaxation of restrictions and art, along with architecture, began to flourish. A local school developed, supplemented by artists from abroad. The first popular form was the portrait, showing the Nantucketer neatly attired in his best clothes, often with a background of his own environment.

By the end of the eighteenth century scenes of the town and island also began to appear. The earliest known is an engraved view of Siasconset. It was executed by David Augustus Leonard and used as frontispiece to his *Laws of Siasconset: A Ballad*, published at New Bedford in 1797 (Figure E). The view is towards the east, with the ocean behind three rows of houses or shacks, about half of which have shed-roof additions or "warts." Among several outbuildings is an elevated granary (lower right corner, a third of the way in) with a ladder or stairs for access. A fence segregates a cow pasture (extreme right), and two cart trails converge on the community (center). In the foreground are four pedestrians, two horsemen, a couple of box carts and three buggies. There is no vegetation of any kind and the scene is bleak.

The second picture presented in the present collection is an oil painting of Nantucket Town attributed to Thomas Birch, a Philadelphia marine artist. It must have been painted no later than 1810, as it formed the basis for the engraving published in the *Port Folio* in 1811 (Plate 2A). Neither tree nor shrub appears in the scene, in which respect the town is like the early village of Siasconset, but what makes Nantucket different is its larger size, its variegated architecture (including windmills and church steeples breaking the skyline), and its diverse topography, with streets and houses on various levels. John W. Barber's view of about thirty years later, from near the same vantage point as the previous two scenes, concentrates on the town and captures its character more carefully than did the Birch (Plate 3).

Earlier than the Barber panorama is the dramatic rendering of the burning of the Washington House on the night of 10 May 1836 (Plate 21). It is a colored lithograph after a watercolor by E. F. Starbuck, who was probably a Nantucket man and a witness to the fire. One feels tempted to identify him as Elisha Starbuck, proprietor of the lost hostelry, but in neither deeds nor other documents does the initial "F" figure in the innkeeper's name, and there is no assurance that the "E" in the artist's name stands for Elisha. Very likely the artist was Edward F. Starbuck (b. 1805), son of Elishai (final "i") Starbuck.

A painting made nearby shortly after the Starbuck lithograph is the view of Main Street looking west from Federal Street (Plate 23). The artist is thought to have been J. S. Hathaway, who flourished during the 1840s and specialized in portraits. A receipt from him to Mrs. Benjamin F. Coffin, dated 1 October 1845, is for three likenesses of her children at $50 each. Hathaway was a primitive, and the picture herein represented is in the primitive style. The list of tenants dispossessed by the Great Fire of 13 July 1846, shows that Hathaway's studio was in one of the three-storied buildings on Main Street at Centre Street (Plate 24). After 1846 his atelier was on the third floor (not visible from ground level) of Allen's Block (43–45 Main Street), over E. T. Wilson's furniture store. Records about some other Nantucket artists are less easily found. Nothing is known, for example, about William H. Gardner except that he must have been one of two males of that name born on the island in 1812 and 1813. He is credited with the drawing from which the sketch represented in Plate 22 was made. The copy was drawn during the last year of the century by George G. Fish, who had studied in Paris and lived in New York before he returned to his native Nantucket (Plate 29).

The Rev. Dr. Ferdinand C. Ewer, although not strictly an artist, produced the historical map of 1869 included in this book (Figure A). Ewer was born on Nantucket in 1826, and after graduating from Harvard College went to California in 1849 and there founded several newspapers and a magazine. He began study for the ministry and became ordained as an Episcopal priest in 1858. Ewer was named rector of Christ Church in New York City, and sometimes officiated at St. Paul's Episcopal Church in Nantucket during visits. Dr. Ewer is remembered for his high-church leanings and ritualistic doctrines. Outside of religion his main interest was Nantucket history, on which he often lectured.

Eastman Johnson, the artist of nationwide fame, also maintained a studio on Nantucket. Johnson was born in Lowell, Maine, and apprenticed to a lithographer in Boston. He returned to Maine to draw likenesses and continued the practice in Washington, D.C., where his sitters included the nation's leaders and their wives. At mid-century Eastman Johnson took up the study of painting at Düsseldorf, and later at The Hague and in Paris. Back in the United States, Johnson spent summers on Nantucket from 1870 to 1887, living on North Shore Hill, where his wife bought land and divided it into cottage lots. The artist's later subjects were grouped in series: portraits, (including those of Indians and Negroes), maple sugaring, cornhusking (both before and during his Nantucket sojourn) and Civil War incidents. He was particularly fond of depicting cranberry-picking scenes; the concluding example of a series of such pictures is reproduced in Plate 16. It was the last of his genre collections, after which he returned to portraiture, depicting the great public figures of his day, such as financial tycoons and two Presidents, Grover Cleveland and Benjamin Harrison.

## NANTUCKET PHOTOGRAPHERS

Many other artists painted the Nantucket scene at the end of the nineteenth and during the twentieth century, but the primary records of the island have been made by photographers. The earliest photograph of Nantucket is a daguerreotype of a section of Main Street (Plate 24). This item is especially remarkable because at that time daguerreotypes were used primarily for making portraits. Furthermore, since the scene does not appear reversed, which is the normal result of the system, the camera must have been equipped with an inverter. There were no known exponents of this photographic method listed among the names of persons or businesses extirpated by the Great Fire of 1846, but in October 1847, an advertisement in the *Nantucket Inquirer* testified to the establishment of "Edward Sutton's Daguerreotype Rooms over the store of Geo. R. Pierce & Co." Pierce's dry-goods shop was the first in the new Hussey Block, on the east corner of Main and Federal Streets. In that period commercial notices in newspapers were limited largely to announcing the receipt of perishable goods or special sales, so the photographer's statement might be considered as signaling the launching of a new enterprise. Edward Sutton either moved about or (more likely) endured competition, for in the spring following the close of the Civil War (1866) an ice-cream parlor announced its opening in rooms "formerly occupied as a Daguerreotype Saloon, over the store of Mr. George Clark" in Orange Street.

By the time of the Civil War photography had advanced considerably and glass-plate negatives were employed, and some of the clearest and best photographs to date were being made. A specialized form was the stereograph, whereby two images of the same scene were produced, taken simultaneously, a few inches apart, and printed and mounted side by side on cardboard. By virtue of the parallax involved, their viewing produced an exaggerated three-dimensional illusion. No less a notable than Dr. Oliver Wendell Holmes invented the hand viewer, or stereoscope, in 1859, and with modifications it remained a much used commodity for over fifty years. Because of the nature of stereoscopic pictures, scenic subjects, especially those involving a vista, rather than people, tended to be the most successful. Prints were generally printed in sepia instead of black and white. The price of slides toward the end of the century was twenty-five or fifty cents.

Nantucket's most prolific exponent of stereoscopic impressions of the town and island was Josiah Freeman. He arrived about 1863 and was at first associated with a local photographer, David Coffin. Three years later, Freeman set out on his independent career. An announcement in the 5 October 1867 issue of the *Inquirer and Mirror*, offered: *"Views of Nantucket, A Large* lot of stereoptic views of the streets and other interesting features of Nantucket just received by *J. Freeman."* His subjects cover a wide range, including vistas of island landscapes and panoramas of the town taken from the church towers (Plates 33–36, 38–40 and 42), shipwrecks (Plates 10 and 12), whales stranded on the beach (Plates 13 and 18), the wharf (Plate 20), street scenes (Plates 45, 48, 73, 76, 93 and 104), studies of individual buildings, both public and private (Plates 5, 27, 46, 47, 50, 72, 81, 83, 88, 90, 95, 102, 106, 125, and 126), a few interiors and details (Plate 91A), and some people (Plate 101). *The Proceedings of the Nantucket Historical Association* announced in 1901 that the organization had purchased a lot of Freeman negatives portraying whaling captains. This prompted Freeman's business successor, Edwin B. Robinson, (Freeman himself retired in the summer of 1892), to sell the Association old negatives of other subjects.

In the Robinson offering to the Nantucket Historical Association were negatives "that appear to date back to the time of Mr. William Summerhays," which would indicate this latter photographer was considered a pioneer in the field on the island. Summerhays had an establishment in the Granite Block, and his sign may be observed in the view of lower Main Street in Plate 44. Summerhays is believed to have specialized in portraits.

During at least part of the 1870–80 period, Nantucket photographers had a rival in C. H. Shute & Son, whose headquarters were on the neighboring island of Martha's Vineyard. Most of the Shute stereographs are relatively early. C. H. Shute & Son's subjects are similar to Freeman's, with shots from across the harbor and from the church towers showing the town (Plate 41), of streets and buildings (Plate 60), some interiors and quaint aspects.

A Nantucketer by birth who took stereographs and offered them on a semiprofessional basis, mostly as a retirement hobby, was Alanson S. Barney. He was born in 1849 and became interested in photography when living in Brooklyn, N.Y. His pictures of Nantucket include views from the church towers, some street scenes and a good many of Siasconset and along the shore. Barney lived at Solid Comfort, a cottage near the Atlantic House on the north side of Main Street, Siasconset. The photograph of the Elihu Coleman house in this book (Plate 7) is stamped "Aug 1904" on the back, but this may be the date when it was printed, rather than the date it was taken. Few stereopticons were produced at this late date. Barney made single pictures as well. His younger brother, William Hadwen Barney (b. 1861), also engaged in picture taking.

After Josiah Freeman, Nantucket's foremost professional photographer was Henry Sherman Wyer. He was born in 1847 and brought up in Roxbury, Mass., and from an early age spent part of each spring and fall on Nantucket. Wyer opened a photographic studio in Yonkers, N.Y., and many of his early Nantucket "cabinet views" give the Yonkers address. His negatives were considerably larger than the usual three-inch-square stereographs. Wyer made a practice of cutting eight-by-ten-inch or seven-by-nine-inch glass plates in half, reducing his negatives to five-by-eight-inches or four-and-a-half-by-seven-inches. His first series must have been taken during the late 1870s, and consisted of: "A large variety of views of Nantucket from the towers and other high places, old houses and other objects of interest." A second series included the first train on the Nantucket Railroad (Plate 111). At that time (early 1880s) his pictures were retailed by Miss E. A. Coleman on Centre Street ("Petticoat Row;" see Plate 73). In 1887 Wyer established a summer residence on the island and opened Wyer's Art Store, where he sold not only pictures but souvenirs and art objects pertaining to Nantucket. He drew and issued a map of the town (including the Cliff area) showing points of interest, hotels and boardinghouses, and it was reprinted in the 25 April 1896 issue of the *Inquirer and Mirror*. Wyer was deeply interested in the island's history and welfare, and was a charter member of the Nantucket Historical Association, organized in 1894. He later served as vice-president of the Association. He also promoted the Relief Association and served on the school board. Wyer was an artist and often combined drawing and photography, as in the spurious scene of whaling boats at the Nantucket wharf (Plate 19), from his *Nantucket Picturesque and Historic*, published in 1901. Wyer earlier had compiled *Poems of Nantucket* (1888) and produced two albums of photographs, *Nantucket in Pictures and Verse* (1892) and *Nantucket: Old and New, Centennial Edition* (1895). The picture of Billy Clark is from the former (Plate 128). Henry S. Wyer's *The Relic Auction* was published at Boston in 1898, and *My Life of Dreams* was issued by the author in 1899. *Sea-Girt Nantucket* came out in 1902, and *Spun-Yarn from Nantucket* was an *Inquirer and Mirror* production of 1914. Wyer pulled up stakes on the mainland and established his residence on Nantucket's Lily Street in 1918. He died two years later. A large assortment of his prints and glass negatives were left to the Nantucket Historical Association, from which collection most of Wyer's many contributions to this book are derived (Plates 6, 31, 37, 43, 51, 56, 57, 59, 61–67, 70, 71, 77–80, 82, 84, 85, 87, 89, 92, 94, 96, 97, 100, 103, 108–111, 118, 121, 123, 131).

Another photographer who worked on Nantucket was Henry C. Platt. Born in 1850 and reared in Augusta, Ga., Platt married a Nantucket Portuguese woman whose family had taken the name of Starbuck. The couple lived in Norfolk, Va., where their children were born during the late 1870s. They visited Nantucket often, though, and late in life lived there. Like Wyer, Platt took glass-plate negatives and often made sepia prints. His subjects were similar to Wyer's, such as the Roberts House (Plate 74), the Sea Cliff Inn (Plate 120), and interiors of the Atheneum and of The Nantucket (Plates 91 and 119). The sheepshearing scene included in this book also bears the Platt name (Plate 14). Most of these photographs are labeled "Platt Brothers, Washington, D.C." The directory of the District of Columbia for 1892 lists Henry and Bernard Platt as residing at 1513 Caroline Street, N.W., and for several other years they have different addresses in Washington. The Nantucket Town records of Henry C. Platt's death in March 1895 characterize him as an artist. His youngest child, Marie, was a graduate of Columbia University and taught art in the New York City schools for many years.

John F. Murphy was collecting or taking pictures on Nantucket at the close of the nineteenth century. Like Wyer, he compiled photograph albums and used some of Wyer's pictures. Murphy's *Fifty Glimpses of Nantucket Island from Photos* was issued by Rand, McNally at Chicago and New York in 1897. It contained the Wyer pictures of the Sherburne House and of The Nantucket included in this book (Plates 67 and 118). Murphy's *Sixty-Five Views of Nantucket Reproduced from Recent Photographs* came out in Boston, undated. The view of the Point Breeze hotel in Plate 121 derives from this source. Murphy also produced *The Tourist Guide, Nantucket and Martha's Vineyard*, no date, and *Views of Nantucket Artists' Colony*, Boston, 1904. He

was responsible for a foldout collection of island vignettes reproduced in two-toned woodcuts, called *Souvenir of Nantucket*, Boston, ca. 1890.

Maurice W. Boyer was born at Fishdale, Mass., in 1875 and came to the island as a child. He learned printing at the *Nantucket Journal* but gave it up in favor of photography during the early 1890s. Boyer was a protege of Henry S. Wyer and took over the studio of Edwin B. Robinson, formerly that of Josiah Freeman, on Main Street. He later moved to Federal Street and ran the Sunshine Shop (a gift and souvenir shop) in conjunction with the studio. Boyer engaged in portraits and scenes (Plate 58), and he also did commercial work and made X-rays at the Nantucket Cottage Hospital. He died in 1938.

Photographic records of Tuckernuck Island were made by Dr. William Sturgis Bigelow, a Bostonian well known in medical and cultural circles. He built a summer home on the islet in the early 1880s, and one picture of its construction is included here (Plate 17).

Another person more active in collecting than taking photographs of Nantucket was Harry B. Turner. Turner was a native, born in 1877, who, while still in school, apprenticed at the *Inquirer and Mirror*. In 1907 he became editor, a position he held until his death in 1948. Turner wrote and published *The Story of the Island Steamers* in 1910, and a chronology of island events, *Argument Settlers*, in 1918, with subsequent editions up to 1944. He edited the newspaper's monumental *One Hundred Years on Nantucket*, issued 27 June 1921, in which appeared the halftone showing horse cars on Brant Point reproduced in Plate 117.

## THE PLATES

The illustrations in this book are divided into several subject groups. The figures for the Introduction are maps and a panorama of Siasconset at the end of the eighteenth century. The first thirty-two plates, "Old Nantucket," are largely of a Nantucket that no longer exists, the exceptions being the mill built by the Nathan Wilbur (Plate 4), the Elihu Coleman house (Plate 7) and the two lighthouses (Plates 8 and 9). The early view of the town seen from a distance (Plates 2, 3 and 30) and the section of Nantucket glimpsed from the end of Old North Wharf (Plate 31) are mostly recognizable, whereas most of the buildings pictured from the streets (Plates 21–27) have been mutilated or demolished, save for the Nantucket Pacific Bank (Plate 23) and the Methodist Episcopal Church (Plate 24). The Jethro Coffin house has been spoiled by an ill-advised "restoration" completed in 1929 (Plate 6), and the Surfside lifesaving station has been greatly enlarged (Plate 11). Shipwrecks (Plates 10, 12 and 13), the appearance of whales (Plates 13, 18 and 20), sheep-shearing and harvesting scenes (Plates 14–16), building a house in the old days (Plate 17) and interiors on Main Street with nineteenth-century clutter (Plates 28 and 29) are things of the past. The beloved *Island Home* exists today only in name (Plate 32), and the scene of whaling ships at Nantucket Wharf was already an extinct phenomenon when the Wyer picture was made (Plate 19).

The section "Views from Two Towers" provides an aerial view of Nantucket. Plate 31, of the Nantucket waterfront at the end of the nineteenth century, shows a glimpse of the First Congregational Church or North Tower, from which the first four views were taken (Plates 33–36). In the last may be seen the upper part of the Unitarian Church or South Tower, from whose summit the following six shots were made (Plates 37–42). The two sets from the towers offer a general idea of what the town was like during the last quarter of the 1800s and prepare one for the surface-level pictures that follow.

Plates 43–98, "Street Scenes and Buildings in Nantucket Town," are arranged geographically. As most of the structures survive, this section may be used as a walking-tour guide. Plates 43–47 are of lower Main Street or the commerical nucleus. Plates 48–55 give a selection of the fine homes on upper Main Street, most of them built by wealth derived from the whaling industry. Plates 56–64 provide glimpses of the south half of the town back to the head of Orange Street. The next five views (Plates 65–69) are of Orange Street, associated with whaling captains and hostelries. By way of Spring (Plate 70) and Union Streets (Plate 71) the tour returns to Main Street.

Plates 72–88 extend up Centre Street and down a number of side lanes from the Methodist Episcopal Church to the First Congregational Church and beyond, as far as Lily Street. An odd house of the late eighteenth century on North Liberty Street is shown in Plate 89, and the final group in this section includes the Nantucket Atheneum (Plates 90 and 91), a vista of Broad Street (Plate 92), and several items on or just off North Water Street (Plates 93–98).

The next sixteen illustrations, "Siasconset and Surfside," explore the village at the east end of the island, Siasconset (Plates 99–110), and the ephemeral boom spot on the south shore, Surfside (Plates 111–114). Another Siasconset scene (at the railroad station; Plate 115) begins the "Transportation" section. In Plate 116 Steamboat Wharf is seen with the railroad terminal in the foreground, and in the next illustration the short-lived horse-drawn railway is shown on Brant Point. The competition of the horse system with the more enduring steam railroad from Town to Surfside and Siasconset is described in the caption to Plate 117.

The succeeding group, "The Great Hotels," pre-sents the three large hotels built in Town during the last two decades of the nineteenth century: The Nantucket (Plates 118 and 119), the Point Breeze Hotel (Plate 122) and the Sea Cliff Inn (Plates 120 and 121). The bathing beach associated with the last is shown in Plate 123.

In "Recreation Centers" several out-of-town refuges are included—the race track at the fairgrounds in South Pasture (Plate 124), the Wauwinet House and the Cedar Beach House at the Head of the Harbor (Plates 125 and 126) and a would-be nearby rival that failed to blossom, Chadwick's Folly (Plate 127).

Plates 128–131 present a few "Interesting People and Events at the End of the Century" two of Nantucket's best known town criers, Billy Clark (Plate 128) and Alvin Hull (Plate 129); and two important events of the late 1890s, the Centennial-bicentennial of 1895 (Plate 130) and the auction of the old windmill on lower Main Street in 1897 (Plate 131).

## NANTUCKET NOW

Today Nantucket Island is becoming built over at the rate of about one hundred houses per year, but Nantucket Town retains considerable charm. Most of its buildings are old and its streets are still irregular, with recently installed brick sidewalks and granite curbs. Houses are more quaint because of additions on the sides and dormer windows on roofs, and many of them have rustic shingles on the walls replacing the original neat clapboards, the latter abandoned because they require frequent painting. Utility wires and street lights (most of them antiquated), radio and television antennae, a modern yacht marina in place of the old wharves that were quiet in their decrepitude, and the summer influx of thousands of automobiles (successfully banned up to 1918) are unfortunate disfigurements of the late twentieth century. But Main Street maintains the old cobblestone paving and is lined with stately elms, and the commerical buildings in its lower reaches and the noble homes in its upper still present a venerable visage. Other streets, lanes and alleys are passageways to the nineteenth and earlier centuries. However, Nantucket is not a museum but a living community. Its year-round population is still below its peak in the early 1840s, and although certain outlying areas have been sprinkled with new dwellings, the town itself has grown little during the last seventy-five years. It retains much of its appearance during whaling days and, except for the supplementing of trees among the housetops, a modern vista of Nantucket is not unlike the earliest views in this book (Plates 2 and 3).

# NANTUCKET
## in the
## Ninteenth Century

# Old Nantucket

**Plate 1. At the Spring on Hinkley Lane, late 19th c.** (Nantucket Historical Association Collection). Beyond the late-nineteenth-century cottage lots northwest of Nantucket Town, Hinkley Lane cuts from Cliff Road out to the edge of North Cliff. At the upper end of Hinkley Lane was a spring where the original settlers and, much later, the summer residents came to get its excellent water. Even after the Wannacomet Water Company began supplying Nantucket houses in the mid-1880s, the spring remained popular. Only the trodden path and beach grass relieve the severity of the bluff that faces Nantucket Sound. Beyond the Sound the nearest towns are Hyannis, Dennis and Harwich Port on the south shore of the Cape, twenty-five miles away.

2  NANTUCKET IN THE NINETEENTH CENTURY

Opposite, top: **Plate 2. Nantucket from the Southeast, ca. 1810** (Oil painting attributed to Thomas Birch, Nantucket Historical Association Collection). In this earliest-known panorama of Nantucket Town, believed to have been painted by the Philadelphia artist Thomas Birch, the community is seen from Shimmo, across the harbor. On the skyline at the left are the four windmills of Popsquatchet Hills, dating from before the American Revolution (Plate 4). Their form is depicted inaccurately here as though they were Dutch windmills. Of the two church towers shown, that to the left is the early one on the Second Congregational Church, erected on Orange Street in 1809. The artist shows it as square and in a plain "Gothic" style. By the time the present tower replaced this one in 1830, the congregation had become Unitarian (Plate 65). The tower with a steeple to the right is that added to the Presbyterian North Shore Meetinghouse when it was moved to Academy Hill in 1765 to serve as the First Congregational Church (Plate 85). The lighthouse seen between the two sailing ships in the harbor is one of a number erected in succession on Brant Point. Its construction seems similar to that of a windmill. The long building nearby is a ropewalk. The Great Point lighthouse, glimpsed in the distance above the tip of Shimmo, is the predecessor of the present light, built about eight years after the painting was executed (Plate 8).

Opposite, bottom: **Plate 2A. The Town of Sherburne in the Island of Nantucket** (Wood engraving by Benjamin Tanner in the *Port Folio*, Philadelphia, 1811, New York Public Library Collection). The Thomas Birch painting evidently served as the model for this engraving by Benjamin Tanner published to illustrate an article by Joseph Sansom in the Philadelphia magazine, *Port Folio*. The use of the name Sherburne is archaic; the name of the town was changed back to Nantucket in 1795. Diminished distances between elements and alterations in the landmarks indicate Tanner was not familiar with the actual subject.

Above: **Plate 3. Southeastern View of Nantucket, Mass.** (From John W. Barber, *Historical Collections Related to the History and Antiquities of . . . Massachusetts*, Worcester, 1839, Atheneum Collection). This engraving was made by S. E. Brown of Boston after a drawing by John W. Barber. The observation point is close to that of the Birch painting, but the scene spans only from two of the windmills to the tip of Brant Point. Aside from the town's normal growth, there are notable differences in the townscape; the Unitarian Church has acquired a new front and tower (center), though the cupola here looks rather like a small steeple, the present First Congregational Church has been built on the site of its predecessor (above the steamboat) and Philip H. Folger's Nantucket Marine Railway (1830) is in operation, indicated by the upright brig and overturned hull to the left of the lighthouse (far right). The ship *Joseph Starbuck* was under construction at the time Barber made his sketch. The steamboat disgorging smoke would be the *Telegraph* (also called the *Nebraska*), which transported passengers between Nantucket and New Bedford. Its destination was later changed to Woods Hole. In the foreground an island box cart proceeds toward the town. The absence of trees is common to all early Nantucket views.

Opposite: **Plate 4. The Old Windmill Seen from Dover Street, late 19th c.** (Nantucket Historical Association Collection). A mill to process grain for bread and pudding was one of the necessities of the original settlement, and in October 1665, the proprietors voted that John Bishop build a horse mill. The following spring the plan was changed in favor of a water mill to be constructed on the stream from Wesco (Lily) Pond. It stood on the site of Chester Street between Centre and North Water streets. But the stream proved too meager for grinding and the mill was used for fulling cloth. Then in 1675, in their last undertaking, the proprietors commissioned Richard and John Gardner and Thomas Macy to build a tide mill "near the place where the mill now stands."

Nantucket once had five windmills. A group of four (depicted in the Birch and Tanner views) stood in a row on Popsquatchet Hills, forming the southwest boundary of Nantucket Town. The easternmost windmill is seen from Dover Street in this photograph. It was erected in 1746 by Nathan Wilbur, and Eliakin Swain was the first miller. One of its companions was torn down,

one burned and one was purchased by the town and blown up to test the destructive power of dynamite, so that this was the only one surviving in 1897, when it was sold at auction to the Nantucket Historical Association (Plate 131). The old mill, now a public museum, still occasionally performs the task of milling.

Above: **Plate 5. The Round-top Mill, New Lane, before 1874** (Stereograph by Josiah Freeman, Atheneum Collection). Nantucket's fifth windmill was built in 1802 to the northwest of Town; on the William Coffin map its location is shown across from the "Burying Ground" (upper left corner, Figure D). Later the cemetery was enlarged to the east side of New Lane, spanning from West Chester Street to the present Franklin Street. The mill stood on the rise immediately south of the intersection of New Lane and Franklin Street. As the name of the mill implies, its vanes revolved from a domed bonnet instead of a triangular turret. The structure was demolished and its millstone used as a foundation for the Civil War monument erected in 1874–75 at Main and Milk Streets.

Top: **Plate 6. Jethro Coffin House, Sunset Hill, before 1886** (Photograph by Henry S. Wyer, Nantucket Historical Association Collection). Built in the eastern reaches of old Sherburne, on the hill above Wesco (Lily) Pond, presumably as a wedding gift in 1686, the home of Jethro Coffin is the oldest house on its original foundations in modern Nantucket Town. Timbers came from land at Exeter, N.H., belonging to Jethro's father, Peter Coffin, who deeded his island property to his son during "the third year of the Reign of Sovereigns William and Mary, King and Queen of England, Scotland, France [William was Prince of Orange] and Ireland," 1692. It is sometimes called the "horseshoe house," from the device on the chimney, which may represent the union of the two principal families of the full-share and half-share factions (Jethro's wife being Mary Gardner) or which may be simply a crude seventeenth-century ornamental arch. The house as built was medieval in style, with leaded casement windows, batten door with strap hinges, a steep roof and twin gables in front (Plate 6A).

The gables allowed the upper rooms to have windows with southern exposure. Although front gables remained unusual, the one-and-three-quarters-story building became a prevalent type on the island. Early in the eighteenth century, the house was modernized to the form shown in Plate 6. The front gables were removed, the pitch of the roof was lowered thirteen degrees and the roof was continued as a lean-to over a new rear extension (shown by the dotted lines in Plates 6A and 6B). Windows were all of the larger sash variety. Horizontal purlins may be seen through gaps in the roof. In 1929, when the house was again refurbished, the lean-to form was kept, but the windows were changed to small casements, even in the rear addition, which never had had them.

Bottom left: **Plate 6A. Original Front (right) and West Elevations, Jethro Coffin House.** Dotted lines indicate the later chimney and roof forms.

Bottom right: **Plate 6B. Original First Floor Plan, Jethro Coffin House.**

**Plate 7. Elihu Coleman House, Hawthorne Lane, 1904(?)**
(Stereograph by A. S. Barney, Richard P. Swain Collection).
Elihu Coleman was the builder of his own house, which was standing on 25 December 1725, when his father, John Coleman, deeded
him an acre surrounding the homesite. His father and a kins-
woman, Jemima Coffin, also each gave Elihu an adjoining acre of
"swamp land." The house stands on a rise to the east of the north
head of Hummock Pond, a little over a mile west of Nantucket
Town. It was the last residence built in old Sherburne and is the
only one still standing in the area. The building is characteristic of
the early-eighteenth-century lean-to—full two-storied in front, and
"double" in size, with rooms on either side of the "porch" and
chimney, a big kitchen in the middle, with a pantry at one end
and borning room at the other, and smaller chambers above. The
principal windows have eight-over-twelve-paned sashes and the
outer doors are batten. Elihu Coleman engaged in other building
on the island. It is recorded, for example, that he worked on the
first Friends' meetinghouse, which stood west and a little north of
his own house.

4088

**Plate 8. Lighthouse on Great Point, ca. 1880s** (Nantucket Historical Association Collection). The first Nantucket ship's beacon, of 1746, was on Brant Point and served to guide vessels into the Great Harbor. It was erected at the town's expense and probably consisted of lanterns hoisted on elevated platforms. Due to the crudity of lamps at that period, the Brant Point beacon burned and was replaced many times. The second shore-light site on the island was at the end of the north spur, Sandy Point or Great Point. In 1785 the federal government built a lighthouse here. The tower was of wood and the light used spermaceti oil. In 1812 the adjacent keeper's-lodge burned and in 1816 the lighthouse itself burned. the present round stone shaft (shown in the photograph) was erected in 1818. It is seventy feet tall and twenty-four feet in diameter at the base and is surrounded by a concentric curb of stones ten feet from the perimeter. The circular newel staircase in the center of the tower has winder steps of four-foot radius. The keeper's dwelling shown was replaced by another at the end of the nineteenth century, and this one was destroyed by fire in 1968.

**Plate 9. Sankaty Lighthouse, late 19th c.** (Nantucket Historical Association Collection). The bluff at the east end of the island had been the site of summer encampments of Indians during their regime on Nantucket; when winter came they forsook it for lower ground inland. From the promontory one looked out on the wide expanse of the Atlantic Ocean and whatever ships or whales might be passing. The highest point is Sankaty Head, just south of Sachacha Pond, where the present lighthouse was erected in 1849–50. It is seventy feet high, on a site one-hundred ten feet above the water. Alexander D. Bunker was the first keeper. With the long sweep of moors leading up to Sankaty Head on the west and the precipitous drop of the bluff down to the sea on the east, it commands a spectacular location. Goldenrod in bloom in the foreground denotes the season as early autumn.

**Plate 10. Bark *Minmanueth* Aground, 1873** (Stereograph by Josiah Freeman, Nantucket Historical Association Collection). The British bark *Minmanueth* beached on Nantucket's south shore near Miacomet Pond on 30 July 1873. It was bound for Boston, carrying four thousand bags of coffee loaded at Rio de Janeiro. The vessel remained upright and immediate arrangements were made to lighten her by removing some of the cargo. Spectators, shown lounging among the coffee bags in the photograph, watch the proceedings. A wagon train carted about one-fourth of the coffee to the Macy store on Straight Wharf in town, and it was forwarded later to its destination by the schooner *W. O. Nettleton*. The *Minmanueth* floated clear but was crippled and had to be towed to the Hub by the steam-tug *J. S. Smith*. Though the bark had to undergo considerable repairs, it was luckier than other ships encountering Nantucket's treacherous south shore. The mishap prompted the location of the Coast Guard's lifesaving station at Surfside.

Above: **Plate 11. Lifesaving Station at Surfside, 1870s** (Nantucket Historical Association Collection). Since the end of the eighteenth century, "humane houses" had been built by insurance companies along the shore at places where wrecks were likely to occur, and the number of such houses was increased considerably by the addition of thirteen during 1831. These houses were supplied with necessities and comforts for the use of shipwrecked men and were the predecessors of lifesaving stations. In the fall of 1873, Charles H. Robinson, who recently had built the first pavilion of the Ocean View House at Siasconset (Plate 106), was commissioned to build a lifesaving station at Surfside for the Coast Guard. The Surfside station was as decorative as the inn, only in the "Queen Anne" or chalet style rather than the Victorian Gothic-cottage style. The bracketed gables at both ends had open timberwork, with cutout dolphins set in the spandrels, and there was a lookout on the roof ridge. The building was larger than the humane houses and it was equipped for active aid to distressed ships. Lifesaving crew members, shrouded in waterproofs which left only the face exposed, resembled space pilots of a century later (Plate 11A). In 1883 lean-tos were added to the flanks of the building and the lookout was converted into a cupola. A facsimile of the Surfside lifesaving station was built at Shawkemo, on the Great Harbor, as a lifesaving museum in 1970.

Left: **Plate 11A. A Crew Member in Lifesaving Gear, 1873–74** (Nantucket Historical Association Collection).

Opposite: **Plate 12. Wreck of the Bark *W. F. Marshall,* 1877** (Stereograph by Josiah Freeman, Nantucket Historical Association Collection). The first wreck to which the crew of the Surfside lifesaving station responded was that of the *W. F. Marshall,* a bark sailing from Hampton Roads, Va., to Saint John's, New Brunswick. The morning of 9 March 1877 was foggy, and surfman Horace Cash, on patrol, spotted the vessel during a moment's clearing. It had run aground on a shoal off the beach near Mioxes Pond, west of the station. Cash summoned the crew, but when they arrived, the boat had disappeared. A warning was fired but received no response. Then the fog parted and the *W. F. Marshall* came into view. The vessel staggered and swung to the side. Breaking waves made it impossible to launch a rescue boat, and a line was shot over the craft so the breeches buoy could be used to bring ashore all on board. They included Capt. James Wright, thirteen seamen, the Negro steward and his wife and six-week-old daughter, and a Newfoundland dog. High winds drove the bark deeper into the sand. The lifeboats, part of the rigging, cables, hawsers, sails and some of the yards were taken off and brought to town. The stranded ship was sold at auction on March 28th for $185 to James Powers of Boston; the spars went for another $25, and the parts that had been removed earlier brought a little more. The initial hopes of hauling off the vessel soon dissipated, however, and what did not go to pieces and get swept away was burned on September 23rd.

Above: **Plate 13. Remains of the *Warren Sawyer* and a Whale, September, 1885** (Photograph by Josiah Freeman, Nantucket Historical Association Collection). On 22 December 1884, the *Warren Sawyer,* a three-masted schooner carrying one thousand one hundred-fifteen bales of cotton and twenty-eight tons of scrap iron from New Orleans to Boston, struck the shore at Surfside about eleven o'clock at night. A patrol of the lifesaving station spotted the ship's light through the mist. They summoned the lifesaving crew, who, by means of the breeches bouy, miraculously rescued Capt. Edwin L. Sanders and his seven men before midnight. An attempt was made to salvage the cargo, but after about seven hundred bales of cotton had been landed, the men were forced to leave; soon the ship was torn apart by an angry sea. Wreckage and cotton bales were churned together in the surf, and men plunged into the frigid water to obtain a prize. The Nantucket Railroad brought the cotton that had been saved to town and it netted about $600. What was left of the ship at Surfside was auctioned for $19. Its bow remained a landmark for many months. And at the beginning of September 1885, a most inscrutable coincidence occurred: the carcass of a whale washed ashore and occupied the exact spot where the hull of the *Warren Sawyer* had gone to pieces.

Opposite, top: **Plate 14. Sheepshearing at the Miacomet Pens, ca. 1890** (Photograph by Platt Bros., Nantucket Historical Association Collection). Raising sheep for wool was Nantucketers' first industry. It determined their early division of the land, whereby small portions went to individuals for homesites, and the greater part was used as commons for sheep grazing. Each shareholder in the proprietary had the right to keep a specified number of sheep, depending on whether he was a full- or half-share member. Sheep raising continued through the peak years of the whaling industry and slowly declined toward the end of the nineteenth century. Sheepshearing was an annual event. There were two shearing pens on the North Cliff, at Maxcy's Pond and at the appropriately named Washing Pond, and there was a third pen on the south shore, east of Miacomet Pond. Sails were stretched over the framework of the pens for shade, as in this photograph, and spread on the ground to catch the fleece. The arduous task of shearing thousands of sheep was accomplished with as much expeditiousness and divertissement as means allowed. Everybody attended, and while some of the men washed and clipped the sheep, the others watched, socialized and feasted. Later shearings ended with a dance in which all participated.

Opposite, bottom: **Plate 15. Salt Haying, Polpis, late 19th c.** (Nantucket Historical Association Collection). Salt haying was an adjunct to both agriculture and cattle raising on Nantucket. The hay was harvested for the animals' bedding in the wintertime, when it would become mixed with manure. When the hay from the animals' quarters was worked into the ground before spring plant-ing, the nitrates in the mixture helped fertilize the soil. Hay was cut in the Salt Meadows (the area between Goose Pond and the wharves in town), in Madaket and in Polpis, on the Great Harbor. In the photograph, oxen are hitched to the box cart, and the farmer in boots and vest carries a pitchfork for the haying.

Above: **Plate 16. The Cranberry Harvest, 1880** (Oil painting by Eastman Johnson, Timken Gallery, San Diego, Calif.). Eastman Johnson (see Introduction) sketched and painted a number of pictures of cranberry pickers in the fields, a series which bears a resemblance to his corn-husking scenes. The cranberry industry on the island started about the middle of the nineteenth century, at the first signs of the decline of whaling, though it did not acquire remarkable momentum until forty or fifty years later. After certain initial difficulties, it was not long before Nantucket could boast of the world's largest cranberry bog (two-hundred-seventy acres) in Gibb's Swamp, in the east quarter of the island. But today, the cranberry industry has practically disappeared from Nantucket.

Johnson was involved in depicting cranberry-picking scenes during the decade following the nation's Centennial. In this painting he combined his various studies of the terrain and figures into a composition of berry-picking groups undulating across the field in front of a backdrop of high ground resembling the North Cliff, where his home and studio stood. The mill on the bank just to the right of the town did not appear in any of the known preliminary sketches: geographically out of context, it was introduced in this version of 1880 as a touch of local color.

**Plate 17. Carpenters at Work on the Bigelow House, Tuckernuck Island, 1884** (Photograph by William S. Bigelow, Nantucket Historical Association Collection). Dr. William Sturgis Bigelow graduated from the Harvard Medical School in 1874 and continued his studies in France under Louis Pasteur. Bigelow was a specialist in septicemia and wrote on it extensively for medical journals. He also spent many years in Japan and delved into the intricacies of Nipponese art, philosophy and religion. Bigelow's interest in the Orient resulted in his writing the popular *Buddhism and Immortality,* published in 1909. He resided at 56 Beacon Street, Boston and commissioned a summer cottage on Tuckernuck. Bigelow recorded its construction and other views of the island. In this photograph three bearded carpenters are shown on the job. One is planing, one sits on a sawhorse and another sits in the rear on a bundle of shingles. The main part of the Bigelow house was two-storied and had walls of vertical planks with weather stripping. A shingled kitchen was under construction in 1884 when the photograph was taken. Bigelow's close friends included Theodore Roosevelt and Henry Cabot Lodge, whom he entertained at the Tuckernuck retreat.

**Plate 18. Boys and Blackfish, late 1890s** (Stereograph by Josiah Freeman, Nantucket Historical Association Collection). The Indians and their English successors on Nantucket engaged in offshore whaling of the smaller variety of whales, called blackfish. They apparently drove the blackfish into shallow water and butchered them. Throughout its history there have also been periodic instances of whales being washed up on the shores of Nantucket; blackfish, in particular, have beached in numbers. Although whales breathe air, they do not have the muscular ability to survive on land, and die of suffocation. During the latter part of the nineteenth century when schools of the animals occasionally became stranded, use was made of the carcasses, even in hotel cuisines. The flesh was reported to taste like a rather dry beef. To the two young island visitors shown in the photograph, a school was the place to relate their thrilling experience of standing on a real whale. And what could have been more opportune than that Josiah Freeman should be on hand to take stereoscopic views for them to show their classmates the sight in three-dimensional reality!

**Plate 19. A Group of Whalers, Contrived before 1901** (From Henry S. Wyer, *Nantucket Picturesque and Historic,* 1901, Atheneum Collection). It is said that in 1690 Nantucketers engaged Ichabod Paddock, of the Cape, to instruct them in better techniques of catching whales and extracting oil from them. In 1712 Christopher Hussey was cruising and was blown off-course and ran into a school of right whales, one of which he killed, and returned to port with its carcass. This incident inaugurated Nantucket's deep-sea whaling. The affluent years of the whale fishery on Nantucket coincided with the period between the American Revolution and the Civil War, the main theater of activity being the Pacific Ocean. The last whaler to leave the island on such an errand was the *Oak,* on 16 November 1869. The ship sent home five hundred ten barrels of oil but did not itself return; it was sold at Panama in 1872. A scene like the one in the photograph, with vessels tied up and endless rows of oil barrels, could have occurred at the Nantucket waterfront before midcentury. This is, however, a fabricated picture and not a true Nantucket scene. The picture may have been created from photographs taken in New Bedford.

**Plate 20. "Cutting In" the Whale at Commercial Wharf, 1870** (Stereograph by Josiah Freeman, Nantucket Historical Association Collection). A dead right whale was picked up by a Nantucket ship off Chatham, at the elbow of the Cape, in the spring of 1870, and the carcass was towed to Commercial Wharf. On April 1st the process of "cutting in" was undertaken, and "everybody and his wife and daughter went down to get a view of the creature." But the odor emitted "was not exactly Arabic Felix," and the spectacle was less nauseous when witnessed from a distance. Josiah Freeman was on hand with his camera and took a number of pictures, including this plate.

A month earlier a right-whale cow with a calf had swum into the Provincetown harbor, at the fist of the Cape. A boat put out from shore and laced the mother whale. She resisted her attackers, who pursued her until late in the afternoon, when the line was cut, allowing the wounded mammal to escape. It would seem from the photograph that the reward for the Provincetown-men's efforts may have fallen to the Nantucketers. The whale shown was sixty-three feet long, and blubber when tried out yielded twenty-two barrels of oil.

**Plate 21. View of the Fire in Main Street, Nantucket, May 10, 1836** (Color lithograph after a painting by E. F. Starbuck, Moore's Litho., Boston, Old Print Shop Collection, New York City). From the southwest corner of the William Rotch Market, we look across the Square and west along Main Street. To the right are the two gambrel-roof warehouses built by Zaccheus Macy and Silvanus Hussey, and George Gardner and several of the Coffins during the mid-eighteenth century. Just right of center is the Zenas Coffin building of 1817, occupied by Thomas A. Gardner's hardware store on the first floor and Thomas Coleman's sail loft above. To the left is the Burnell Store, between Washington and Union Streets, and over the upper rake of its curb roof may be seen the dome of the Unitarian Church cupola (Plate 65). Enveloped in flames are Francis F. Hussey's home and store, and Elisha Starbuck's inn, the Washington House. The bases and

pedestals of the latter's portico pillars show below the billowing smoke. The inn was created in 1831–32 by enlarging Betsy Cary's boardinghouse. The hostelry's spacious hall and numerous guest rooms made it Nantucket's finest. The fire started in the Washington House's kitchen chimney about eleven-thirty at night, and within two hours it had destroyed not only the Washington House and Hussey buildings on Main Street, but two stores around the corner on Union Street. Two hand pumps are in operation, and the kneeling figure and his helper in the center have the supply hose fed into the fire cistern that was installed opposite Water Street in 1833. Other men are carrying buckets of water, and a few are taking valuables to safety. This fire burnt only four or five buildings. The one that followed ten years later consumed one-fifth of the town.

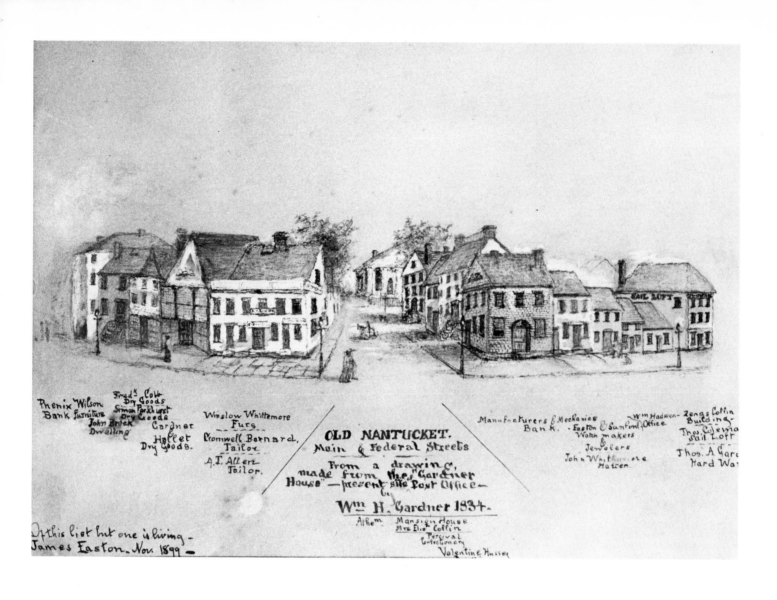

The handwritten labels on the drawing read:

Phenix Wilson
Bank furniture
John Brock
Dwelling

Fred's Coit
Dry Goods
Simon Parkhurst
Dry Goods
Gardner
Hallet
Dry Goods.

Winslow Whittemore
Furs
Cromwell Bernard,
Tailor
A.I. Allen
Tailor.

OLD NANTUCKET.
Main & Federal Streets
From a drawing
made from the "Gardner
House" —present site Post Office—
by
Wm H. Gardner 1834.

Athem     Mansion House
          Mrs Eliz. Coffin
          Percival
          Confectionery
          Valentine Hussey

Manufacturers & Mechanics
Bank    Easton & Sanford, Office
         Watch makers
           &
          Jewelers
        John Whittemore
           Hatter

Wm Hadwen  Zenas Coffin
          Building
            Thos. Coleman
            Sail Loft
          Thos. A. Gardner
          Hard Wa[r]

Of this list but one is living—
James Easton. Nov. 1899—

**Plate 22. Main and Federal Streets Before the Great Fire of 1846, 1899** (Drawing on tinted paper by George G. Fish, 1899, Nantucket Historical Association Collection). George G. Fish (Plate 29) inscribed his sketch as having been made, "From a drawing . . . by Wm. H. Gardner 1834." The Gardner drawing would have to be later than 1834, however, as the Atheneum portico had not been added at that time, the white building on the corner of Main Street had not been remodeled as shown, and the structure next to it, the Gardner & Hallet store, had not been built. At the far right of the drawing is the front of the Zenas Coffin building, the east side of which figures prominently in the 1836 fire scene (Plate 21). There is some confusion regarding the next two little buildings, as only a single small store (rented by William Hadwen for his "mechanical" operations) actually existed between the Coffin building and the Philip Pollard house. The third house from the corner of Federal Street was built in 1746. Adjoining its west side (towards Federal Street) is the Valentine Hussey building of 1823. On the corner of Federal and Main Streets is the Manufacturers' and Mechanics' Bank, constructed of brick in 1825. The building behind the bank was the home of Josiah Gorham, erected by him in 1820. The little house beyond was built

for Josiah Barker before 1800, and housed the Pacific Bank from 1804 until 1818, when the bank moved to its own headquarters on Main Street (Plate 47). The large three-story building with pediment at the front was the Federal Street House, constructed or enlarged from an existing structure by Nathaniel C. Cary in 1832, and run by his brother, Samuel. During the early 1840s it was Mrs. Elizabeth C. Coffin's Mansion House, as it is so identified on the drawing. The building farthest up Federal Street is the old Atheneum, originally constructed to serve as the Universalist Church in 1825, but remodeled eleven years later for use as a library and museum (Plate 25). On the west corner of Main and Federal Streets (left of center) stands the late-eighteenth-century William Macy house. It was modernized in 1836 for commercial purposes by Josiah Gorham. Adjoining it is the Gardner & Hallet store, built in 1835. The next building is the Lydia Macy store, dating from some time between 1805 and 1811 and used for business purposes from the latter date onward. To the left of this store is a Quaker-type house and two adjoining three-story buildings that can be seen distinctly in the daguerreotype of Main Street (Plate 24). Most of the tenants of the buildings during the early 1840s are identified on the drawing.

Above: **Plate 23. Main Street, Looking West from Federal Street, 1840–46** (Painting attributed to J. S. Hathaway, Atheneum Collection). J. S. Hathaway was a primitive painter of portraits who rented a studio in the right-hand block until it was destroyed by the Great Fire of 1846. The first two buildings in this block correspond fairly well with their images in the Fish copy of the Gardner drawing (Plate 22), except here they have acquired shelters over the sidewalks. The three-storied Nantucket Bank building, whose corner shows beyond, can be seen more fully in Plate 24. Facing us is the Nantucket Pacific Bank of 1818 (Plate 47). In the foreground, on the left side of Main Street, is the Gardner (boarding) House, which had the post office on the ground floor. Photographs made of the painting before it was "restored" about 1960 seem to indicate stairs to the basement of the house. The red-brick house depicted practically in profile is that of Philip H. Folger, built at the west corner of Orange Street in 1831 (Plate 46). Homes on Main Street beyond are identified in the northwest view from South Tower (Plate 42). Several trees shown indicate that there were predecessors to the American elms planted along Main Street at mid-century.

Left: **Plate 24. North Side of Main Street and Liberty at the Centre Street Intersection, early 1840s** (Daguerreotype, $2\frac{1}{2} \times 2\frac{5}{8}$ inches, Nantucket Historical Association Collection). This daguerreotype, the earliest known photograph of Nantucket, was made during the early 1840s, and it has belonged to the Nantucket Historical Association since at least 1896, two years after its founding. The daguerreotype is particularly valuable because it shows Main Street before the Great Fire of 1846. The first building on the right was the late-eighteenth-century home of Jonathan Macy, occupied from the 1830s on by Dr. John Brock II, barber and peruke-maker. It is a four-bayed Quaker or typical Nantucket house-type. The three-storied building next to it was erected for the Nantucket Bank in 1806. At the time the picture was taken it was occupied by Adams' and Parker's grocery and E. T. Wilson's furniture store. The sign over the door of the latter reads: "Furnishing Warehouse." The building between it and the corner was Samuel Bigelow's double dwelling of 1804. Beginning in 1818 it housed the Nantucket Phoenix Insurance Company, and in 1839 it was acquired by the Nantucket Institution for Savings, a bank still in existence, though now called the Nantucket Savings Bank. On the far side of Centre Street is the Methodist Episcopal Church, built in 1823, with the portico added in 1840 (Plate 72). To the left of the head of Liberty Street is the Nantucket Pacific Bank. This photograph must have been taken from the upper story of Washington Hall, which replaced the Washington House, burned in 1836 (Plate 21).

Right, top: **Plate 25. The Old Atheneum, Federal at Pearl (India) Street** (From John W. Barber, *Historical Collections Related to the History and Antiquities of . . . Massachusetts,* Worcester, 1839, Atheneum Collection). Originally this building was the Universalist Church, whose cornerstone was laid on 1 May 1825; the church itself was dedicated on November 3rd, with the Rev. Josiah Flagg preaching. It was rectangular and plain except for a pointed doorway and windows in the "Christian" (Rococo Gothic) style. The site on which the church stood was not deeded to the proprietors of the congregation until 17 July 1827, and at least part of the deeded land was fifteen feet narrower than the building itself. There was, however, a strip of common land (probably too irregular to be desirable for private ownership) on the east side of the church, so no problem arose. On 6 August 1834 the property was sold to Aaron Mitchell for $3,500, and on the same day Mitchell deeded it to Charles Coffin and David Joy for only $1,800, although there were undoubtedly other unrecorded considerations. At the beginning of 1836 Coffin and Joy, who stated in their deed the desire "to promote the Cultivation of Literature, the Sciences and the Arts, and thereby advance the best interests of our Native Town," gave the building for the Nantucket Atheneum, a public library and cultural center. The Roman Ionic tetrastyle portico was added then to the facade, and changes were made inside to provide a "commodious Lecture Room" and "spacious and convenient rooms for the library . . . and the deposit of curiosities, principally from the Pacific seas." The building and most of its contents were destroyed by the Great Fire of 1846. The present building rose on its foundations (Plate 90).

Right, bottom: **Plate 26. Trinity Church, Broad Street** (From the *Nantucket Inquirer*, 14 September 1839, Atheneum Collection). This charming little Gothic Revival building stood next east to the Ocean House (Plate 83) on Broad Street. It originally was the North Meeting branch of the Friends, after the old meetinghouse at the corner of Main and Grave Streets (Quaker Road) had been pronounced "inconvenient." In 1793 or 1794 half of the congregation went to the "South" house at the Main and Pleasant Streets intersection and the other half here. When the group on Broad Street moved to Fair Street in the mid-1830s, the old building was opened for public use under the name of the Broad Street Hall. The Episcopalians began worshipping here on Sundays. They later purchased the ground with the thought of building their own church; but the oak frame of the Broad Street Hall was found sound, so it was moved back on the lot and became the basis of a new forty-five-by-sixty-five foot auditorium. It was given tall, "gothicized" windows in the flanks, buttresses with pinnacles at the corners, crenelations atop the walls and a square tower in front. Over the Tudor-arched doorway were a pointed window, clock section (the clock itself never materialized) and tall lancet openings filled with louvers in the belfry section. Pinnacles capped the

angle buttresses, as on the building proper. Walls were of wood, and were "coated with plaster and Roman cement; the whole covered with a mixture of paint and sand, colored to resemble granite." Designed and supervised by C. Pendexter, Trinity Church was dedicated on 18 September 1839. It was a casualty of the Great Fire of 1846.

Opposite: **Plate 27. Eben Allen Cottage, Broad Street, late 19th c.** (Stereograph by Josiah Freeman, Nantucket Historical Association Collection). In 1840 the "Wardens, Vestry and Proprietors of Trinity Church" mortgaged the Broad Street property for $400 to Thomas Thompson. A year after the Great Fire of 1846 had destroyed the original building, Thompson foreclosed for the land. In 1866 Thompson sold it for $750 to Eben Allen, owner after 1857 and proprietor after 1864 of the adjoining Ocean House (Plate 83). Allen built and occupied the cottage shown in this plate. The residence partook of the quaintness of post-Civil-War eclectic architecture. Buildings in this style were mushrooming on Martha's Vineyard, but very few were built on Nantucket, and most of these did not appear until the 1870s. The main feature of this cottage was the dipping mansard roof, overspread with lozenge designs in colored slate, pushed up into which were round-headed dormer windows. Eaves were supported on coupled brackets. The front veranda, though rather plain, is of the same period as the rest of the building; it may have been the builder's personal contribution to the design. Eben Allen sold the Ocean House in 1872 and died four years later. During the early 1890s the cottage was let by Mrs. J. D. Nesbitt. In 1897 it was sold by the executor of the estate of Mrs. Allen to Fitzhugh S. Rollins. The cottage was torn down soon after World War II, and replaced by an annex and terrace to the adjoining hotel.

Above: **Plate 28. The Union Store, Main Street, late 19th c.** (Nantucket Historical Association Collection). The large brick building constructed after the Great Fire of 1846 at the intersection of Main and Centre Streets was called the Union Block, from its amalgamation of four stores. When it opened in March 1847 the grocery of Bradley and Chase occupied the corner stand. At the end of the century the unit shown in the photograph was still a grocery, now called the Union Store. During the 1890s illumination was by electricity, with naked light bulbs suspended by wires from the ceiling. A meat-chopping block stands in the center of the room, and a refrigerator dominates the left wall, with brooms offered for sale on the front end and a stuffed mountain lion (not for sale) on top. Ceramics are stacked on the rear cabinet, and in the far right corner are bags of coffee and a grinder. Canned and packaged goods line the shelves along the right wall. Royal Baking Powder containers form a pyramid in the right foreground. The Union Store also featured King Arthur Flour and Kennedy's Biscuits.

**Plate 29. George G. Fish in His Studio, late 1890s** (Nantucket Historical Association Collection). George G. Fish was born on Nantucket in 1825. His ambition to study in the art capital of the world was fulfilled in 1866 when he and his wife, Judith Derrick, sailed for France. Fish took up the neoclassic manner of portraiture, presumably under a master named Brochart. Their first child was born in Paris and named Madeleine after the early-nineteenth-century church near which they sojourned. The family returned to America and for about thirty years resided in New York City, where George specialized in portraits. In the mid-1890s they came back to Nantucket, and Mrs. Fish conducted a boardinghouse on Broad Street from 1895 onward (Plate 92). The artist engaged the West Room in the Atheneum as a studio, and later worked above Charles Lovell's store on Main Street, where he is shown in this photograph. Fish preferred a dry (pastel or crayon) medium to paint. His subjects are idealized and posed in rustic settings. Often his drawing and composition are faulty because his attention is focused on a finished technique. Examples of his work (belonging to the Atheneum) may be seen over the mantels in the public rooms of the Jared Coffin house, and he drew the scene in Plate 22. Fish was well versed in English literature, a subject on which he often talked and sometimes lectured; he was also proficient as a violinist. He died in 1906.

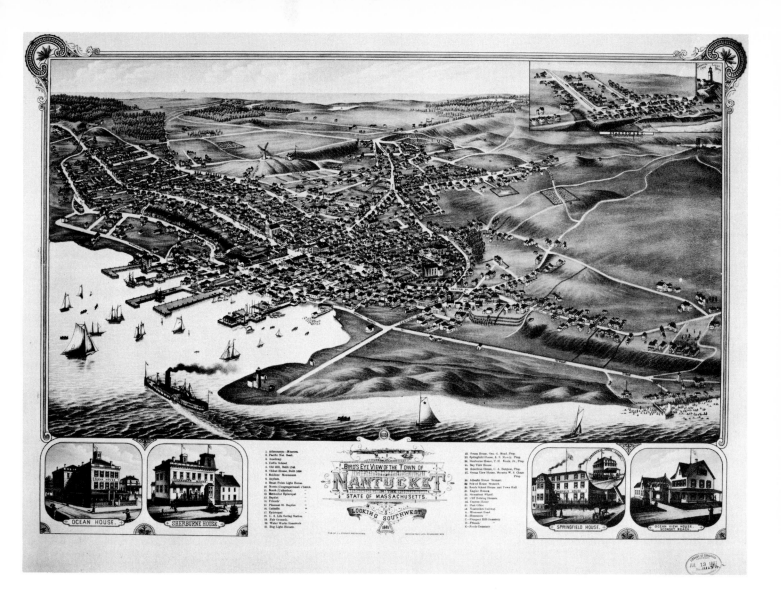

Above: **Plate 30. Bird's Eye View of the Town of Nantucket, July 1881** (Lithograph by Beck & Pauli, Milwaukee, Wis., published by J. J. Stoner, Madison, Wis., Library of Congress Collection). The community is seen from above the entrance to the Great Harbor, looking toward the southwest, and with the view extending from the fairgrounds (upper left corner; see also Plate 124) to the junction of North Liberty Street and Cliff Road, with North Cliff and the Cliff Shore beach below (lower right corner; see also Plate 123). Most of the town is shown in an enlargement in Plate 30A (over). The street meandering diagonally between these two locales is made up of Orange, Centre ("Center" on this view) and then Cliff Road (here "North St."). Of the five large piers protruding into the harbor, the middle one is Straight Wharf, on a line with Main Street, which curves up to the Civil-War monument (a bit above exact center; No 7 on the plate), beyond which it extends almost horizontally to the right. Dark shadows denote the rise of Quanaty Bank or Wesco Hill (above the harbor on the left) and North Cliff (near the bathing beach on the right). Rising over the lower end of Quanaty Bank is South Tower (No. 11 on the plate; see also Plate 65); directly above it is the Baptist Church (No. 13; see also Plate 60); to the right of South Tower, across Main Street, is the Methodist Episcopal Church

(No. 12; see also Plate 72); and North Tower, embraced by the arc of Lily Street (No. 10, right of center; see also Plates 31 and 85) is a little beyond the Methodist Episcopal Church. The old windmill (No. 5; see also Plate 4) is on a slightly diagonal line up from South Tower. Crossing Orange Street (extreme left), disappearing into the pine grove and emerging onto the sheep commons, are the tracks of the Nantucket Railroad, headed toward the south shore. In the foreground of the scene the *River Queen,* bringing summer visitors, is rounding Brant Point, headed for Steamboat Wharf (Plate 116). This facsimile of the lithograph, accepted for copyright on 13 July 1881, is the only one examined by the author that does not depict a train on the line. The rolling stock (Plate 111) had not yet reached the island when this early impression was pulled. Copies for sale were received at Nantucket around July 20th and could be purchased for $2.00. In the upper right-hand corner is a box containing a sketch of Siasconset that includes horsecars on Main Street that were proposed but never realized (Plate 117). Below the view of Nantucket are four vignettes of the leading hotels.

Over: **Plate 30A. Detail of Plate 30.**

Above: **Plate 31. The Waterfront from Old North Wharf, late 19th c.** (Photograph by Henry S. Wyer, Nantucket Historical Association Collection). Toward the end of the nineteenth century the quay section of Nantucket looked quite different from the way it had forty years earlier (Plate 19). The mercantile clutter of whale products and tall square ships had been replaced by a relaxed serenity and small graceful fishing or pleasure boats. Wyer's picture shows that part of town between Old North and Steamboat Wharves. Above the treetops, about a third of the way in from the right, is North Tower, the First Congregational Church (1834), minus its steeple, from which the views in Plates 33–36 were taken. The plain buildings in front are commercial structures at the foot of Broad Street. The curve of pilings at the water's edge skirts the tracks of the Nantucket Railroad (Plate 111), which had its terminal on Steamboat Wharf from the mid-1880s through 1917 for the convenience of passengers arriving or departing by ship. In the cove are a number of catboats, distinguished by their triangular hulls, broad at the back, and their shallow draw for navigating among shoals and close to the shore. The mast for the single spanker sail is set well forward. Catboats could be rented for fishing or conducting passengers to Wauwinet and other points on the Great Harbor. The exceptionally large catboat, *Cleopatra* (left), sporting an American flag for sail, was owned by George W. Burgess.

Right: **Plate 32. The *Island Home*, late 19th c.** (Atheneum Collection). Nantucket's link with the mainland by steamboat got off to an uncertain start in 1818 with the little eighty-ton *Eagle* making trips between the island and New Bedford. Service lasted three months. Ten years later an even smaller boat (fifty tons), the *Hamilton*, steamed over the same route with no better success. In 1829 the one-hundred-forty-ton *Marco Bozzaris* followed, and trips continued until the fall of 1832. She was replaced by the one-hundred-seventy-one-ton *Telegraph*, whose construction was coeval with the founding of the Nantucket Steamboat Company, 4 February 1833. In 1842 the *Massachusetts*, twice as large as the *Telegraph*, was built as an alternate steamboat for the New Bed-

ford trips. Later (1854) the *Massachusetts* operated to and from Hyannis. In 1854 a New Bedford concern began running a ship called the *Eagle's Wing* to Nantucket, and the following year a consolidation of interests between Nantucketers and Hyannis capitalists resulted in the Nantucket and Cape Cod Steamboat Company, and the construction of the *Island Home*. This was a five-hundred-thirty-six-ton ship, whose machinery was manufactured by the Morgan Iron Works of New York; the vessel itself was built by the New Haven Steamboat Company. The *Island Home* was a luxury liner, with velvet-covered furniture and marble-topped tables, and, it was said, in her, "Nothing was wanting to promote the comfort of the travelling public." Like her predecessors the *Island Home* often lent assistance to vessels in distress, which was not unprofitable to the owners. She made the run to Hyannis until 1872, when the destination was changed to Woods Hole. The steamer ceased to serve Nantucket in 1895, when she was sold and converted into a coal barge.

During the late 1880s the boardinghouse of Mrs. E. B. Harps on Cliff Road bore the ship's name. Now it is memorialized in the name of the Nantucket domicile for the elderly, "Our Island Home."

# Views from Two Towers

**Plate 33. View from North Tower, Looking Northwest, late 19th c.** (Stereograph by Josiah Freeman, Nantucket Historical Association Collection). The long rear slope of the lean-to roof of the Benjamin Chase house (mid-eighteenth century), moved here from Fair Street in 1810, occupies the center of the foreground facing Lily Street. The white house with four chimneys to the main block, directly above, is the enlarged Thomas Gardner residence of 1739, standing on Gull Island, which was originally surrounded by Lily Pond. In this view, however, the pond has receded and is out of camera range to the south. From the 1880s onward the Gardner residence was Mrs. H. L. Riddell's board-inghouse. The smaller white house on Gull Island (left of center) was later moved to the lane at the right. The next road back is West Chester Street, which connected old Sherburne with the Great Harbor long before the present Nantucket Town materialized. The farthest house in the center group (with black chimney) is the Jethro Coffin house (Plate 6). It is truncated at the rear by a fire that destroyed the northeast room. Its nearest neighbor on Sunset Hill was the Nathaniel Paddock house (early 1720s), now gone. The lean-to house near the left margin, below West Chester Street, was built for Richard Gardner about 1722-24.

Opposite, top: **Plate 34. View from North Tower, Looking North, before mid-1880s** (Stereograph by Josiah Freeman, Nantucket Historical Association Collection). Lily Street, flanked by the two white fences in the foreground, terminates at Centre Street (right) between the shingled duplex (center) and lighter building beyond (left of center). The latter was Swain's boardinghouse from the 1870s onward (Plate 88). The house beyond its chimney, at the corner of Chester Street, became William J. Chase's guesthouse in 1874. At this point Centre Street divides, the left fork becoming West Centre Street (now called West Chester Street) and the right fork (now North Centre Street) connecting with North Street (Cliff Road) at the top of the rise. The small lean-to to the left of the junction of North Street and the right fork of Centre Street is the house of Nathan Folger, which was standing when his father, Barzillai, gave him the property in 1775. This vista was made before the Sea Cliff Inn (Plates 120 and 121) and summer cottages sprang up along the road at the crest of North Cliff.

Opposite, bottom: **Plate 35. View from North Tower, Looking East, before mid-1880s** (Stereopticon by Josiah Freeman, Nantucket Historical Association Collection). At the time this picture was made the old lighthouse and its satellites were the only structures on Brant Point. The lighthouse was built in 1856 to replace a series of predecessors erected on this site since 1746, and it was to be replaced by the present one in 1901. After the failure of Philip H. Folger's marine railway (established in 1830), no construction existed along the waterfront between the lighthouse and Steamboat Wharf until Charles E. Hayden built the Clean Shore Bathing Rooms in 1869, enlarging them in 1876. The north end of the bathing establishment is visible in the upper right-hand corner of the photograph. The large, three-story house at the left, facing Centre Street, is the Peter Folger II "flat-roofed house,"

built in 1765 and altered about fifty years later (Plate 84). The road descending the incline, on the right, is Step Lane. Buildings on the north side of Step Lane were to become hostelries. The front porch of the third house from the corner was later expanded, thus giving title to the Veranda House (Plate 98). The lane continuing beyond is the present Sea Street, which joins South Beach Street. This region, including the remains of Hayden's bathhouses and the early twentieth-century Athletic Club, currently is occupied by the Yacht Club.

Above: **Plate 36. View from North Tower, Looking Southeast, late 19th c.** (Stereograph by Josiah Freeman, Nantucket Historical Association Collection). Many houses along Centre Street, above its bend at Broad Street, feature the Nantucket roof walk. It originated as a scuttle in the roof adjoining the chimney, as a means for pouring a bucket of sand or water down a flue that might have caught fire; and it developed into a platform with a railing around it, serving as a lookout for sighting vessels entering the harbor. The size of roof walks varied from the limited standing place, such as on the duplex house at the bottom of the picture, to the entire length of the roof ridge, as on the white residence across the street. Note the false upper facade of the shed-roofed extension of the last-named, its prop clearly visible. The brick building next (center) is Jared Coffin's residence, built in 1845, which became the Ocean House two years later (Plate 83). Its crowning cupola is the enclosed mansion-version of the platform lookout. At the left may be seen the pilastered flank of the Atheneum of 1846-47 (Plate 90). The south curve of the Great Harbor is beyond. The row of large buildings, just above center, is the commercial nucleus on lower Main Street (Plate 43). On the skyline at the right is the Unitarian Church or South Tower on Orange Street, from which the next six photographs were taken.

Above: **Plate 37. View from South Tower, Looking North, late 19th c.** (Photograph by Henry S. Wyer, Nantucket Historical Association Collection). This vista is directed straight up Centre Street to the Jared Coffin mansion, with the First Congregational Church (North Tower) seen beyond, to the left. At the base of Centre Street are the Pacific National Bank building, here painted a light color (Plate 47), and behind it the Methodist Episcopal Church (Plate 72). The rear of the Philip H. Folger house, at the corner of Orange Street (center foreground), has a curved wall to accommodate the double parlors and chamber above: the front of the house with two similar curves can be seen in Plate 46. The roof walk at the bottom of the picture is atop the gambrel roof of the Silas Jones house (Plate 65). The white Greek Revival house across the street from it no longer exists. American elms line the broad stretch of lower Main Street, the east end of which figures in Plate 38. The south end of Federal Street joins Main at the right edge of this picture; in Plate 38, Federal Street is at the left side of the picture.

Opposite, top: **Plate 38. View from South Tower, Looking Northeast, 1870s** (Stereograph by Josiah Freeman, Nantucket Historical Association Collection). Frame buildings along the south side of lower Main Street were constructed hastily after the Great Fire of 1846, and they lacked the pretentiousness of the brick row opposite (Plate 44). Note the false fronts, center left, masking the gables toward the street. In this early picture Hussey's Block retains its original parapet above the cornice, and the rounded bay at the corner of Federal Street contains windows; the lower window opening later became a doorway. The white building behind the Block was that of Dr. David G. Hussey,

dentist, dating from 1864. Beyond it is glimpsed the roof of Harmony Hall, built slightly back from Federal Street for meetings of the Sons of Temperance in 1846; in 1858 the Hall became the Catholic Church. These two frame buildings were removed from the site for the erection of the present Saint Mary's in 1896. The Hussey house then was used first as a restaurant on Steamboat Wharf and later as a summer cottage at Beachside. Beachside was the north shore of Brant Point, which appears in the picture as a dark strip parallel to the skyline. Moored at Steamboat Wharf is the *Island Home* (Plate 32).

Opposite, bottom: **Plate 39. View from South Tower, Looking East, late 19th c.** (Stereograph by Josiah Freeman, Nantucket Historical Association Collection). The far half of the lean-to house in the center foreground was built for Solomon Gardner soon after 1717, when the Fish Lots were laid out, extending inland from Quanaty Bank. The near side of the house was added and occupied by Paul Gardner in 1755; the other parts came later. Like all early houses on the island, the building is oriented toward the south, though this makes it turn its back on nearby Main Street and leaves only Gardner Court and the little crooked Stone Alley at the front for access. Houses below, toward the quay, face Washington and Union Streets, the latter bent, bringing the two into close proximity at their north end. Most of the buildings beyond replace predecessors destroyed by the Great Fire of 1846, which devastated the waterfront almost down to Commercial Wharf (top right). In the upper left, Old South Wharf and (far left) Straight Wharf jut out into the water, with Coatue across the Great Harbor.

Opposite, top: **Plate 40. View from South Tower, Looking South, late 19th c.** (Stereograph by Josiah Freeman, Nantucket Historical Association Collection). Orange Street, at the brink of Quanaty Bank, was the stronghold of whaling captains during the first half of the nineteenth century and of hostelries after the Civil War. Beginning in the right-hand corner are the roofs of Philip's Block (Plate 66). The house whose roof is visible beyond the Block is that of Isaiah Nicholson, housewright, built about 1819. The white one next (upper stories visible) is that of Josiah Gorham, also a builder, dating from 1844, perhaps a remodeled building. The dark building with the two chimneys (north corner of Martin's Lane) was a boardinghouse from the winter after the Great Fire of 1846 throughout the nineteenth century. It was run first by Mrs. Thompson, then the Myricks and Adeline Fanning; it became the American House of Charles A. Burgess and finally the Holiday Inn of Charles H. Robinson, who added to and elaborated the building. It and the storehouse with gable at the front, opposite, (the second building beyond the house with the two dormer windows) have been razed. The building beyond the tree on the left side of Orange Street is the Adams House, later the Sherburne House (Plate 67). The building with a cupola around the bend of the block is the Bay View House (Plate 68). Stretching southward in the background are the sheep commons.

Opposite, bottom: **Plate 41. View from South Tower, Looking Southwest, 1870s–80s** (Stereograph by C. H. Shute & Son, Nantucket Historical Association Collection). This intimate view of the town's backyards, with their kitchen gardens, wash lines, privies and other outbuildings, overlooks the lower reaches of the Fish Lots. In the lower right-hand corner is St. Paul's Episcopal Church, built facing Fair Street in 1849–50, the successor to Trinity Church on Broad Street (Plate 26) and on the site of the present Episcopal Church, built in 1901. Beyond (center and left), a public way leads in from Fair Street to the alley behind the houses here and those facing Orange Street. The three-storied house with hip roof at the right edge of the plate was built for Capt. Obed Starbuck in 1831, and the next house for Thomas Coffin II in the late eighteenth century. The one-story pedimented

building four doors down from the Coffin house was the mid-nineteenth-century Fair Street Academy (south corner of Charter Street, now moved to Quince Street; see Plate 81). Above the school is Nathan Wilber's windmill (Plate 4). The brick house with cupola faintly distinguishable in the upper right-hand corner is Moor's End, built in 1829–34 for Jared Coffin before he moved to Broad Street.

Above: **Plate 42. View from South Tower, Looking Northwest, 1870s** (Stereograph by Josiah Freeman, Nantucket Historical Association Collection). In the lower right-hand corner of the plate is the rear of the lean-to house built for Benjamin Gardner shortly after 1727 at the north end of Fair Street, and across from it is the mid-eighteenth-century residence (probably originally also a lean-to) of Paul Gardner. Both have been demolished. Defunct as well are the two white clapboard houses flanking the brick on the far side of Main Street. That to the left was built for Mrs. Alice Swain, and that to the right for Capt. David Thain, the Philadelphian active in getting congressional support for the construction of the jetties, begun in 1881. The two houses date from 1871, and they were the first off-islanders' summer homes built in Nantucket. A year later a third summer house was constructed for Mrs. Eliza Barney, next left of the Swain house, only the top of whose superstructure is visible here. The brick house was erected in 1834 for Frederick Mitchell, and the other brick residence farther up the street was the home of Henry Coffin, built in 1832–33 (Plate 48). The white house on the near side of Main Street was that of John Wendell Barrett, built after 1831; it has the finest cupola in Nantucket (Plate 48B). Just beyond it, at the far left, protrudes the corner of the late entrance pavilion to Atlantic Hall, originally a Friends meetinghouse (1831) and then a straw-hat factory, which was moved to Brant Point to become the main block of the The Nantucket (Plate 118). Halfway between the town and skyline, a quarter of the way in from the left side of the plate, the Round Top Mill is faintly distinguishable (Plate 5). The large building in the upper-right-hand corner is the mid-nineteenth-century school on Academy Hill.

# Street Scenes and Buildings in Nantucket Town

**Plate 43. Lower Main Street, East from the Corner of Orange Street, early 1890s** (Photograph by Henry S. Wyer, Nantucket Historical Association Collection). Wyer's photograph was taken soon after the William Rotch Market, at the far end of Main Street, originally a light color (Plate 45), was painted red in the spring of 1891. A tangle of electrical and telephone wires detracts from the Square, the venerable elms serving as poles for the crossarms. Beginning at the left-hand corner, on the north side of the street, Covil & Pease's market is in the east end of Allen's Block, Crosby's grocery is next to it in the Lydia Macy store, and the Troy laundry and a barber are in the pilastered brownstone building of Kelley and Gorham on the west corner of Federal Street. The *Nantucket Journal* office is over the Periodical Depot across Federal Street, on the east corner. Several markets occupy the balance of the Hussey Block. The Abial Coffin store at the end of this block housed George E. Mooer's auction house after it moved from Union Street in 1879 (Plate 131). Almost all of these buildings were sponsored by the people who owned the structures burnt in the Great Fire of 1846, even though those on the old narrow Main Street stood in front of the present sites (Plates 22–24). The *Inquirer and Mirror* office is on the upper floor of the building at Orange Street, the first building on the right-hand corner. Charles Lovell's store, a barber, optician, watchmaker, grocer and the Post Office occupy consecutive stands down the block.

Above: **Plate 44. The South Side of Lower Main Street, 1870s** (Nantucket Historical Association Collection). Except for the two-storied brick building of Harvey Crocker and George H. Riddell at the corner of Orange Street (see Plate 43), structures built after the Great Fire of 1846 in the long south block extending to Union Street were low and shoddily constructed. When these buildings were demolished at the end of the nineteenth century, wreckers marveled that they had remained standing fifty years. At the right in this view is the E. G. Kelley building, containing five shop units. Its thick wood piers and deep entablature were originally painted to resemble stone, and the row assumed the name of the "Granite Block." Of its initial (1846) tenants, the Post Office remained here throughout the century. In this 1870s view signs over the street indicate that William Summerhays, photographer, has taken over what had been the Commercial News Room and office of the *Nantucket Inquirer*, and a shoe-repair shop has replaced A. M. Nahar's hair-dressing saloon. The next building to the left of this Block—before the Great Fire of 1846 the site of the Washington House (Plate 21) and, later, Washington Hall—was L. Dexter's boardinghouse and restaurant during the 1870s. After that, the building served as the second Washington House of J. B. Watkins and, still later, it was Roberts' Restaurant and Bakery (Plate 131). Shops at the end of the block are in the Francis F. Hussey building, which was replaced in 1890 by the Masonic Hall (Buttner's now downstairs).

Opposite, top: **Plate 45. The Northeast Corner of the Square, Lower Main Street, 1870s** (Stereograph by Josiah

Freeman, Nantucket Historical Association Collection). After the Great Fire of 1846 some of the streets in Nantucket Town, including Main Street, were widened (see Introduction), and the first two stores on the left of this plate are the only buildings on the north side of lower Main Street built on the exact site of their predecessors. The stores were commissioned by Philip H. Folger. In the second store on the ground floor was the Union News Room, with the *Inquirer and Mirror* (known before its amalgamation with the rival newspaper in 1865 as the *Nantucket Weekly Mirror*) occupying the second floor until the newspaper moved to the corner of Orange Street in 1887 (Plate 43). The twin gables of the two stores were combined into the present jerkin-headed roof about 1902. The next building was built for Grafton Gardner and Henry T. Defries a few feet west of its predecessor's site, as South Water Street was broadened and Coal Lane was reduced to an alley. The two sections were combined into a single store for Pease & Ayers in 1915. The brick building whose side is partially obscured by the tree is the William Rotch Market (1775), half of which was used by the town in exchange for having given Rotch the land on which it stood. In 1831 the Commerical Insurance Company bought and occupied the building. After the Great Fire of 1846 the company refurbished the empty shell, changing the doorway and windows and adding the full third story in place of the original gambrel roof. The Pacific Club, for retired sea captains, bought and further modified the building in 1861. The club still maintains its headquarters here.

Opposite, bottom: **Plate 45A. Restored West Flank and Facade Elevations, William Rotch Market.**

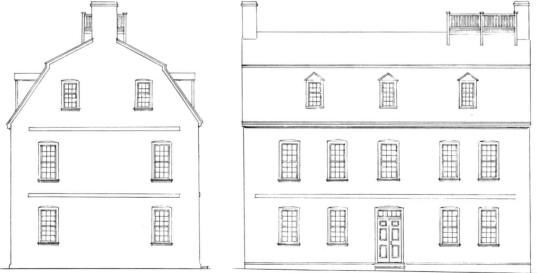

Opposite, top: **Plate 46. Philip H. Folger House, Main at Orange Street, late 19th c.** (Stereograph by Josiah Freeman, Nantucket Historical Association Collection). When it was intact, the home of Philip H. Folger was the handsomest residence in Nantucket. Folger bought the Orange Street corner on 18 February 1831 and had an existing house removed. His new residence reflected the materials and roof form of the bank opposite (Plate 47), but the facade sported a decorative whorled frieze and curved walls in the manner of Asher Benjamin's work on Beacon Hill, Boston. To this basically Federal design were added several Greek Revival elements, including the brownstone portico (of a correctly proportioned Doric order), window labels of the same material and a wooden parapet at the summit of the truncated hip roof. Folger was no longer residing here when he converted the lower part of the house to commercial purposes immediately after the Great Fire of 1846. The floors on either side of the hall were lowered to street level, the walls were torn out for shop fronts, and iron posts (like those used in the Atheneum at the same time) were inserted to sustain the upper masonry. The original elaborate plasterwork of the great parlor with curved ends may still be seen in the west store's frieze and centerpieces. When fire damaged the roof in 1925 it was removed and replaced by a flat covering, and the chimneys were abridged to half their former height. An iron fence to either side of the front steps matched the railing on the Pacific Bank.

Opposite, bottom: **Plate 46A. Restored Front Elevation, Philip H. Folger House.**

Above: **Plate 47. The Pacific National Bank, late 1860s** (Stereograph by Josiah Freeman, Nantucket Historical Association Collection). The Nantucket Pacific Bank is the finest example of pure Federal-style architecture in Nantucket. Built of Flemish-bond brickwork on granite foundations, with brownstone and wood trim and a slate roof, its windows are set in blind arches in the first story and recessed panels above. The portico was originally semicircular, though during much of the nineteenth century it was replaced by the enclosed rectangular vestibule shown here. The podium, at least, remained half-round, with brownstone steps enclosed by iron railings flaring out in graceful curves. When the bank moved here from the corner of Federal and Cambridge Streets in 1818 (Plate 22), only the east (front) pavilion existed. Soon afterward a three-bay extension was added along Main Street, with a small court between it and another rear wing. The early name, Nantucket Pacific Bank, was changed to the Pacific National Bank in 1865; about the same time the building was given a bracketed cornice. Toward the end of the nineteenth century two bays were added to the south side, and further alterations in the north wing in the late 1920s brought the building to its present dimensions.

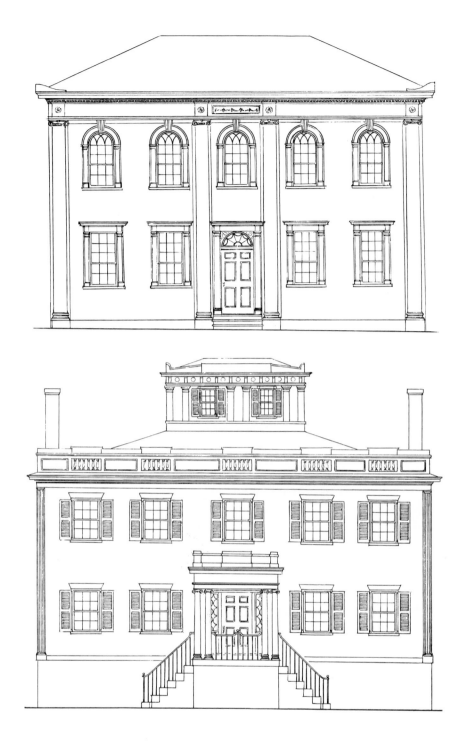

Opposite: **Plate 48. Main Street, West from the Pacific National Bank, late 1860s** (Stereograph by Josiah Freeman, Nantucket Historical Association Collection). The Classic frame building beyond the bank is the Masonic Lodge Hall (second building from the right), built in 1802. During the 1830s its original tall Roman Ionic pilastrade was cut away at the base and replaced by Greek Revival shop fronts. The William Barney house is shown in this late-1860s view next to the Masonic Lodge Hall. In 1870 or 1871 two bays at the west (far) end of the lodge hall were demolished to accommodate the David Thain house, which replaced the Barney house, and at that time one of the deleted pilasters was inserted between the arched upper windows of the remaining portion of the lodge hall. The Thain house and Frederick W. Mitchell brick residence of 1834 (next house) may be seen in the northwest view from South Tower (Plate 42). At the bend of the street is the Henry Coffin brick residence of 1832–33,

whose garret is a veritable museum of whaling memorabilia. Between the two bricks is the white clapboard house of Sarah Bunker (1821). On the left is the home of John Wendell Barrett, president of the Pacific Bank from 1848 to 1867; the house itself was built after he acquired the land in 1831. The limestone obelisk at the curb near the bank's doorway (fourth curb post from the right) is the north meridian stone, whose south companion is in front of the Friends schoolhouse on Fair Street. The meridian stones were erected in 1840 by William Mitchell, the bank's cashier, and amateur astronomer and father of the more famous Maria (Plate 58).

Top: **Plate 48A. Conjectural Restored Front Elevation, Masonic Lodge Hall.**

Bottom: **Plate 48B. Front Elevation, John Wendell Barrett House.**

Above: **Plate 49. The William Hadwen Houses, Main at Pleasant Street, ca. 1870s** (Atheneum Collection). William Hadwen was a native of Newport, who came to Nantucket from Providence, married Joseph Starbuck's daughter and engaged in various enterprises, beginning with silversmithing and concluding with whale products. In 1840 Hadwen bought and remodeled No. 100 Main Street and was living at that address when he purchased the lot on the east corner of Pleasant Street in November 1844. He engaged Frederick Brown Coleman, architect of the nearby Baptist Church on Summer Street, to design his residence. In the spring of 1845 Hadwen bought the adjoining lot on Main Street and had the same architect conceive a house for his niece and adopted daughter, Mrs. George (Mary G. Swain) Wright. The two buildings were the only two private residences in Nantucket to have colossal-order porticoes, and their yards were framed by the appropriate fences shown. Both houses have cupolas, and originally they had elaborate parapets above the cornices. Hadwen's own home is five-bayed and has a tetrastyle Ionic portico. In the 1920s the present balustrade around the Hadwen house was

erected to replace an intermediary iron-rail fence. The Hadwen house is now a museum.

Opposite, bottom: **Plate 49A. Portico Detail, Wright House.** The Wright house is a narrow prostyle form, with an elaborated Corinthian order whose capitals derive from those of the Tower of the Winds in Athens, but they combine anthemia, rather than grasses, with acanthus leaves. Modillions as well as dentils are included in the entablature. Inside the Wright house there are domed ceilings, niches, pilasters and door heads in the style of Minard Lafever; the house was refurbished in 1927. Parts of the original fence remain.

Above: **Plate 50. The Three Bricks, 93, 95 and 97 Main Street, ca. 1890s** (Stereograph by Josiah Freeman, Nantucket Historical Association Collection). The brothers Charles G. and Henry Coffin had set the precedent for fine brick houses farther down Main Street (Nos. 78 and 75) during the early 1830s. Their homes employed the same plan, though inverted as they were on opposite sides of the street, with the main rooms oriented alike, yet external details were somewhat different. Joseph Starbuck visualized building identical residences for his three sons, and

purchased land for them opposite Pleasant Street in 1835 and 1836. Starbuck engaged James Childs, a house carpenter from Cotuit, and Christopher Capen, the mason who had built the Coffin houses, to carry out the work within the next two years. The three two-story houses were of brick, on granite basements, with stone lintels and slate roofs. Ornamental features consisted of small, distyle Ionic porticoes, parapet balustrades and square cupolas on top. Starbuck was a Quaker, however, and as one might expect from a Quaker, the style of his houses was conservative: a transition from Federal to Greek Revival. It is interesting that Jared Coffin's residence on Broad Street, although built six years later, employed identical motifs in a three-story building, except that the wider center bay had triple windows over the portico (Plate 83). The three houses on Main Street had slight differences inside, and, in October 1850, Joseph Starbuck gave the "West Brick" to his oldest son, George, the "East Brick" to the second son, Matthew, and the "Middle Brick" to his youngest, William. The sidewalk in front is paved in bluestone. Today only the West Brick (here the farthest-away of the three, and barely visible) retains its early Gothic-style cast-iron fence.

Above: **Plate 51. Thomas Macy House, 99 Main Street, late 19th c.** (Photograph by Henry S. Wyer, Nantucket Historical Association Collection). Eunice Coffin brought the early version of the house shown on the left of this plate to Thomas Macy upon her marriage to him, 8 September 1824. Nine months earlier, Eunice's father, Zenas Coffin, had purchased it from Valentine Swain for $432. At that time it was a "typical" (Quaker) Nantucket house of four bays. Thomas Macy, who had risen from being a blacksmith to a shareholder in several whaleships, added fourteen feet to the west end of the building, converting it to a two-chimney residence with a central transverse stair hall. A continuation of the stoop railing to an entire front fence, the doorway topped by a fan (which is blind), a triple window over the door, the balustrade insets over windows in the parapet atop the modillion cornice, and the roof walk combine to make a highly satisfactory design. The builder has achieved such attractive proportions that the result is more pleasing than similar houses built all at one time, such as the Matthew Crosby house (1828) at No. 90 Main Street. Thomas Macy had only a life interest in the house, and upon his death the ownership reverted to a daughter, Mary S., wife of Valentine Hussey II.

Opposite: **Plate 52. Isaac Folger House, 110 Main Street,** **late 19th c.** (Nantucket Historical Association Collection). In 1853 Isaac H. Folger bought a rather narrow lot on upper Main Street just west of Isaac B. Hussey's, beyond which was the Nantucket Town House at the corner of Milk Street. The residence constructed for Folger was clapboarded, with thick pilasters at the corners and a deep full entablature all around. Four evenly spaced windows were at the front, and above them a great pointed opening rose from the horizontal cornice to the apex of the pediment. A small piered entrance portico was on the east side, and four tall chimneys flanked a parapeted cupola set on the ridge of the roof. The picture here shows the dormer windows that were added later, and some newly planted trees at the curb, with striped wooden guards around their trunks. The handsome equipage in the street probably belonged to the Cathcart family, who owned the house from 1879 until the end of 1896. Afterward, the pediment window was replaced by a round-headed Palladian, which required removal of a section of the horizonal cornice so that the new window could be placed lower in the wall. In another later attempt to "early" up the style of the house, the dormers were given slender pilasters and smaller-paned sashes. Today, the portico has been expanded into a good-sized porch, and the chimneys and cupola have been removed.

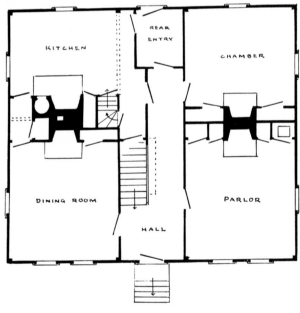

the eighteenth century. This type had abandoned the old center chimney for a transverse stair hall, and its chimneys were situated between the front and back rooms on either side, which plan resulted in manifold improvements in circulation and heating. The spaces about the chimneys also provided convenient closets, a bake oven and service stairs, and a narrow passage to the west of the kitchen chimney had a service window to the front half of the house which permitted food to be handed through to the dining room. Fireplace walls in both front rooms and the space under the stairs in the hall are paneled. Of twenty-nine houses of the two-chimney type surviving in the town, only the Cary house and the three-storied Obed Starbuck house (1831) on Fair Street (Plate 41) have hip roofs, called "Dutch cap" in Nantucket. The Starbuck house may have been modeled on the Cary house; and the latter's doorway, a later alteration, may have been copied from that of the former.

Left: **Plate 53A. Restored First Floor Plan, Edward Cary House.**

Opposite, top: **Plate 54. George Wendell Macy House, 123 Main Street, late 19th c.** (John W. McCalley Collection). George W. Macy's first claim on the lot and house of Elizabeth Clasby on Main Street was an 1842 mortgage, and in the spring of 1844 he was given a clear deed to the property. Macy remodeled and greatly enlarged the old dwelling in the Greek Revival idiom. The original one-and-three-quarter-storied form was embellished with pilasters at the corners, entablatures on the flanks and an unusual one-column portico on the east side. Macy added a kitchen ell and a narrow one-story projection containing half the entrance stair hall and dining room. The original parlor and stair hall at the front were combined into the new and enlarged parlor, which was heated by a stove rather than a fireplace. The west bay of the room is spanned by a steamboat-gothic arch, which supports the fireplace in the smaller vaulted chamber above. The outside door to the service ell is sheltered by a tiny porch sustained by a

Top: **Plate 53. Edward Cary House, 117 Main Street, ca. 1900** (From an H. Marshall Gardiner postcard, Atheneum Collection). The executors of Bethuel Gardner sold Edward Cary the "House Lot Land" of two hundred eighty-nine rods, facing south on the "Main East & West Road," for £77/1/6 on 14 November 1788. The deed stated that it was a part of "Crooked Record, granted to the Gardner family." Cary built a two-story house belonging to a type proper to the island during the second half of

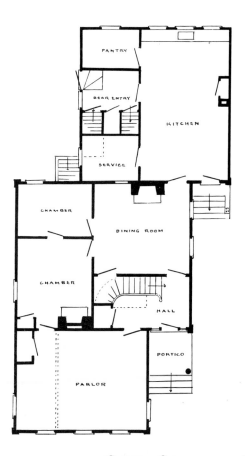

cluster of slender colonnettes, and the eaves above are pushed up into a steep gable by a triangular-headed window. These romantic external details were in the style of the parlor arch. A cupola, barely visible in the photograph (toward the street, obscured by the tree) has been altered, and shingles now replace the old clapboards on the walls of the house.

Above and right: **Plates 54A and 54B. Front Elevation and Restored First Floor Plan, George Wendell Macy House.**

Above: **Plate 55. George C. Gardner House, 141 Main Street, 1870s** (Nantucket Historical Association Collection). In selling George C. Gardner "Two Acres & twenty six Rods & 9/10 more" for $1,000 on 11 October 1834, James Athearn described the tract as a "Certain Lot of Mowing Land bounded on the South by a highway." The "highway," of course, was upper Main Street. The acreage was part of the Crooked Record grant of 1673 to Richard Gardner, the new owner's great-great-great-great-great-grandfather. George C. Gardner's residence was the work of John Gardner, who also built the Sanford house on Federal Street, on the site of the present Town Building. Both houses are clapboarded, on high brick basements, and have five-bayed facades, small distyle Ionic porticoes at the entrance and two tall chimneys on each end. The Sanford house, downtown, was a story taller, whereas Gardner's residence had a roof walk from which one could see the harbor, before trees screened the view. On the right of the plate may be seen the Gardner slaughterhouse, which was blown down by a gale in 1880, and to the left is the barn of Gardner's next-door neighbor, Asa Coffin.

Opposite, top: **Plate 56. The Old Jail and House of Detention, Vestal Street, late 19th c.** (Photograph by Henry S. Wyer, Anonymous Private Collection). Isaac Coffin's Nantucket survey of 1799 listed Prison Lane as beginning at Milk Street, proceeding by the "south side new Poor House to Grave Street." The last-named is now Quaker Road. William Mitchell's deed of 1818 referred to his house as fronting the "street which leadeth to the County Gaol" (Plate 58). William Coffin's map of 1834 (Figure D) established the name once and for all as Vestal Street. The jail, located toward the west end, set back from Vestal Street, midway between it and Main Street, was built in 1805, or very

likely reerected from another site. It is unique on the island in being of log construction. The logs have been squared, laid horizontally and notched together at the corners. The insides of the walls are sheathed with iron straps and the windows are latticed with iron bars. The building is covered with shingles outside and has an external staircase. The larger house of detention, dating from 1826, was originally at Quaise and was moved and placed next to the east end of the jail in 1854, perhaps replacing the "Poor House." The later building was demolished in 1954, at which time the jail already had shifted from a felon to a tourist trap, its inspection requiring a small fee. The present stocks are modern. The sort of discipline they represent played no role on Nantucket.

Opposite, bottom: **Plate 57. The Starbuck Shop, 8 Vestal Street, late 19th c.** (Photograph by Henry S. Wyer, Nantucket Historical Association Collection). On William Coffin's 1834 map of Nantucket (Figure D) the shop on Vestal Street is shown in outline with a rear wing extending to Green Street. On August 18th of that year Simeon Starbuck sold it for $1,000 to John G. Whippey, who took a $750 mortgage with Starbuck at the same time. The mortgage was paid off on 2 March 1844, but for some unexplained reason Starbuck resumed ownership on 1 January 1847, for $209.60. Whippey was a block maker and must have used the building for his profession for more than a dozen years. Later it was known as the cooper shop, and it is said to have contained steam-powered machinery. In 1900 the building passed from Thaddeus Bunker to Thomas S. Ceely for $50. Ceely restored and reproduced antiques, specializing in inlay work, until his death in 1914. The shop currently is a summer home.

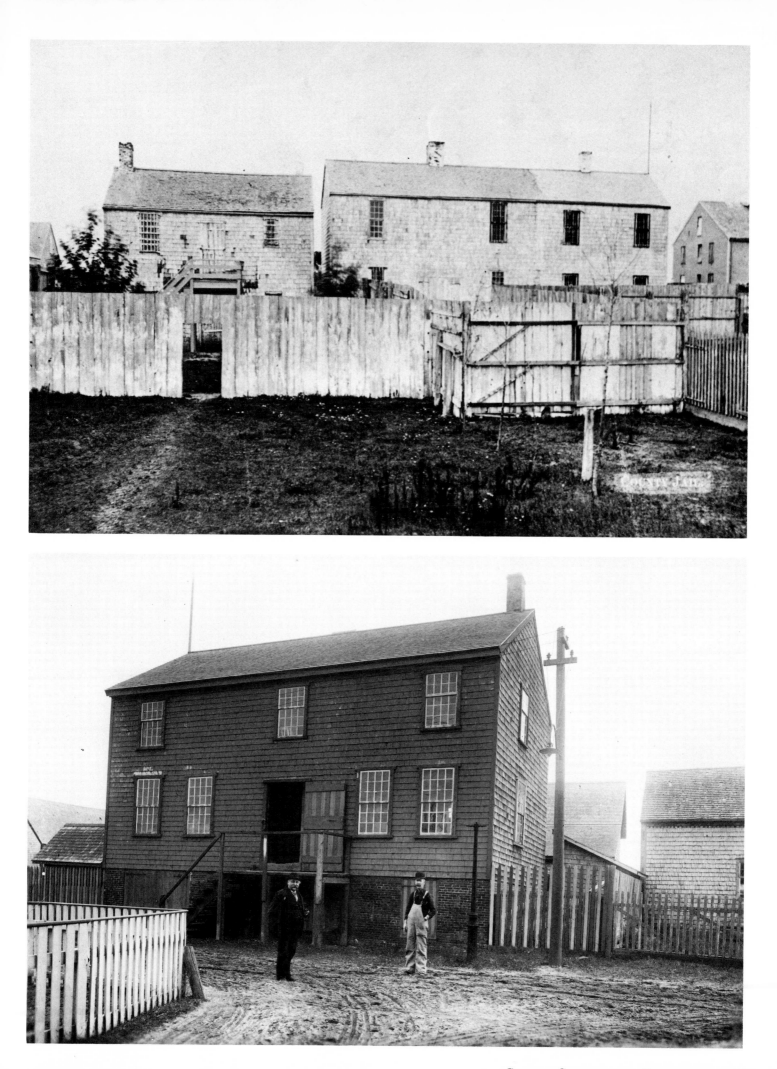

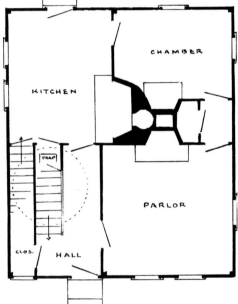

Above: **Plate 58. Vestal Street, the East End, late 19th c.**
(Photograph by Maurice W. Boyer, Anonymous Private Collection). In this photograph cows are heading out from Milk Street along the muddy lane that leads to pastures west of town. The first house on the left is now gone, and an observatory built in 1908 takes its place. The second is said to have been built by Hezekiah Swain in 1790. It was a simple squarish Quaker house, typical of the period, which was acquired by Simeon Gardner in 1815. Gardner was a housewright and probably added the present rear ell. He sold the building to Aaron Mitchell in 1816, and, at the beginning of 1818, Aaron resold it to his second-cousin, William Mitchell. The latter's daughter, Maria, was born here on August 1st of that year. Maria Mitchell distinguished herself in the field of astronomy and was a professor of the subject at Vassar College. When asked once if she did not think that female delicacy was unfit for the irregular nocturnal hours required by her prime interest, Miss Mitchell replied in her deep sonorous voice: "Sir, my mother had more night work than astronomy will ever demand of any woman. She brought up eight children." The house is now part of a science complex and is open to the public as a museum.
Right: **Plate 58A. Restored First Floor Plan, Hezekiah Swain House.**

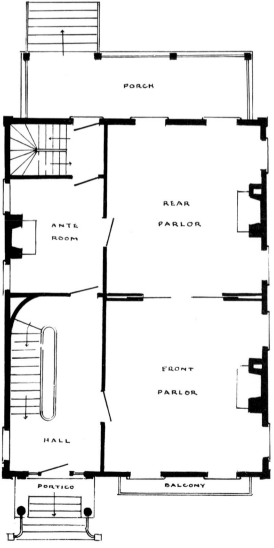

Above: **Plate 59. William H. Crosby House, 1 Pleasant Street, late 19th c.** (Photograph by Henry S. Wyer, Nantucket Historical Association Collection). When Alice Bernard sold her home on Pleasant Street to William H. Crosby in the spring of 1835, the old Friends meetinghouse (1792) stood on the west corner at Main Street, though it was not being used, and was owned by Henry and Charles G. Coffin. A year later Crosby bought a narrow strip from the meetinghouse lot to enlarge his yard. At that time the owner was Benjamin Coffin, who sold Crosby the meetinghouse as well, and the building was then moved to the head of Commercial Wharf to become the Crosby & Sons candle factory. In 1837, Henry Macy built a new house (shown in the photograph) for Crosby. It was not large, measuring less than thirty by forty feet, but it was given an inordinant amount of elegance. Like a city house, the dining room and kitchen were in the basement. Most of the first story was occupied by twin parlors, which were lighted by eight tall windows rising from the floor, each containing triple sashes in the architectural manner of Thomas Jefferson. Those in front opened onto an iron balcony—a unique feature in Nantucket—and those opposite onto a back porch. The entrance is sheltered by a portico of two Doric columns, and the hall contains a graceful staircase with open well leading from the basement to the chamber floor. A small room with fireplace was behind, and service stairs in the southwest corner of the building connected basement to garret. The building has an unusually steep roof for a pediment treatment in front: the roof does, however, permit an ample third floor. The cupola on the slate roof is similar to those on the neighboring Starbuck and Hadwen houses. During the late nineteenth century the Crosby house was enlarged at the rear. Recently it has served as an inn and is now an art gallery.

Left: **Plate 59A. Restored First Floor Plan, William H. Crosby House.**

**Plate 60. Baptist Church, Summer Street, ca. 1870s**
(Stereograph by C. H. Shute & Son, Nantucket Historical
Association Collection). The Baptist Society of Nantucket purchased the lot at the corner of Summer Street and Trader's Lane
for $200 on 8 August 1840. Frederick Brown Coleman was engaged
to design a church. His original scheme is reported to have included a portico, but this feature was deleted as an unnecessary
expense. As built by John Chadwick the building is rather plain,
with paneled pilasters across the front and at the corners supporting a simplified entablature, and pediments in front and in back.
The tower of several stages with steeple was added in 1841, and a
bell was installed in 1854. To the left of the church (beyond the
corner of No. 7 Summer Street) is the rear end of the carriage house
to No. 92 Main Street, and to the right of the Baptist building may
be seen South Tower on Orange Street. Today fixed colored-glass
windows supplant the early clear-glass sashes in the Baptist
Church, and the top of its tower was replaced by an exact copy in
1962.

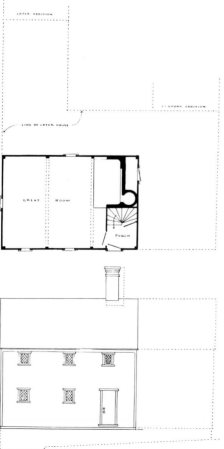

Above: **Plate 61. Parliament House, 10 Pine Street, late 19th c.** (Photograph by Henry S. Wyer, Nantucket Historical Association Collection). John Folger, an early-nineteenth-century Quaker carpenter, is said to have told his grandson that he incorporated "material from . . . the home of Mary and Nathaniel Starbuck" in the double house on the north corner of Pine and School streets. The Starbuck dwelling was built about 1676 just west of the north head of Hummock Pond, and was called the "Parliament House" because of meetings held in it. There is no question about the framework being seventeenth-century in that part of the Pine Street building beginning at the northwest corner (on the left of the photograph) and extending thirty feet along the front and running twenty feet deep, Members have chamfered edges and lamb's-tongue cuttings, and they embraced a single large room on each floor besides the enclosed "porch" and stairway. The house at No. 10 Pine Street originally had been the Charles Bunker "settlement" in the Fish Lots when John Folger purchased three-eighths of it (the south section) in 1819 and the rest in 1824. After the latter transaction it would seem that Folger rebuilt the part adjoining his own assembled residence, moving and using the old framework of the Bunker house. Each unit of Parliament House also has the remains of an old round cellar in the modern basement. Upper windows are smaller than those below. The optical effect of perspective that this creates and the elevation off the ground give the illusion the building is much larger than its actual size.

Left: **Plate 61A. Restored Front Elevation and First Floor Plan, Nathaniel Starbuck Dwelling.** The dotted lines show their relationship to the form of the Pine Street building.

Opposite, top: **Plate 62. John F. Nicholson's Houses, 32–34 Pine Street, late 19th c.** Photograph by Henry S. Wyer, Nantucket Historical Association Collection). Twin Street was nameless in the spring of 1840 when John F. Nicholson, housewright, paid Levi Starbuck $420 for an irregularly shaped lot at its intersection with Pine Street. The land measured fifty-four feet across the front. Over the next eight weeks Nicholson built a little frame cottage on a high brick basement, and on May 2nd he sold it, along with twenty-three feet of the Pine Street frontage, to William Perkins, mariner, for $1,000. Nicholson then set out to erect a larger residence on the greater adjoining strip. The house was standing by the summer of 1841 when he mortgaged it for $1,000. In the spring of 1844 Nicholson had not repaid the loan when he sold the property to Nathan Walker, painter and glazer, for $250, plus assumption of the mortgage. The two houses maintained unity by having clapboarded facades, pilasters at the doorways and corners of the buildings, supporting entablatures, and similar windows; they achieved distinctiveness by having differences in form, both in size and in the positions of roofs. The modern deletion of classic dress from the larger house, the addition of an inappropriate Dutch dormer to the smaller, and the replacing of neat clapboards with rustic shingles drives home the value of maintaining simple and well-handled architectural details for proper scale and dignity.

Opposite, bottom: **Plate 62A. Modern View, 32–34 Pine Street.**

Above: **Plate 63. Benjamin Robinson House, 37 Fair Street,** late 19th c. (Photograph by Henry S. Wyer, Nantucket Historical Association Collection). The building whose rear may be seen at the left in the photograph, between the two residences facing Fair Street, is the Thomas Macy homestead, built soon after the Fish Lots were laid out in 1717. Macy's share (lot No. 19) lay between the present Darling Street (at the right) and Tattle Court (which the house faces) and extended from Fair to Pine Street. Characteristically for the period, the house is oriented to the south, and is a lean-to type, full two-storied in front. The Macy lot was divided many times. Seth and Benjamin P. Coffin bought the northeast corner in 1822. Five years later they split it and Seth sold the Fair Street side to Benjamin Robinson in 1831. Robinson was a builder and constructed the house facing us. Since it does not figure on William Coffin's map of 1834 it must have been built later. It retains the center-chimney plan but is raised on a full basement. The pilastered doorway and narrow, half-round window frames with board lintels having splayed ends are features of the late Federal or early Greek Revival period. Window sashes are six-paned (some of them replaced in this late-nineteenth-century picture), and walls are clapboarded on all sides. The open spiked parapet is an interesting variation. Benjamin Robinson's son, Charles H. Robinson, was also a builder who constructed the Surfside Lifesaving Station (Plate 11), the Dunham house on Orange Street (Plate 65), the Sea Cliff Inn (Plate 120), and summer cottages and his own Ocean View House at Siasconset (Plates 105 and 106).

**Plate 64. Double House, 29–31 Fair Street, late 19th c.**
(Photograph by Henry S. Wyer, Nantucket Historical Association
Collection). Daniel, John and Caleb Bunker acquired three-
fourths of Fish Lot share No. 18 in the partitioning of 1717, and
fifty years later their heirs divided the land. The descendants of
Daniel received the east part, and George Bunker's homestead site
was at the north corner, adjacent to what eventually became
Hiller's Lane. George built a two-story, lean-to half-house, and
when a second house was attached later (probably around 1800) to
its south flank, the lean-to was heightened to two full stories at the
back, with the roof taken up to a new ridge behind the chimney.
The pilastered doorway and clapboards on the front date from the
same time. The newer house (left) followed the same plan as the
old, with winder stairs in front of the chimney, parlor at the front
and kitchen at the back. Posts and beams were no longer exposed
inside, though, and window panes had increased in size. The
Bunkers kept the corner house until a little before World War I,
after which it became an inn. The two buildings were united in
1931, and they continue to exist under the name of the Wood Box.

**Plate 65. Jones and Dunham Houses and South Tower, Orange Street, late 19th c.** (Photograph by Henry S. Wyer, Nantucket Historical Association Collection). No other houses in Nantucket are more different from one another than these two, built a century apart. The first on the right of the photograph was already the home of Silas Jones when, on 3 May 1776, he and two neighbors divided land hitherto held in common. The only local building to which this house relates architecturally was the William Roch Market (1775) on lower Main Street (Plate 45A), and they must date from about the same time. Both buildings had gambrel roofs and they are unique in the eighteenth century in being of brick with chimneys on outside walls. Actually, the Silas Jones house originally was of brick only on the ends, having clapboards in front, as still exist in back. The brick facade dates from the 1830s and marks an advance in the early wall plane, precluding a full cornice overhang in front. The doorway with transom and sidelights as well as the windows with six-paned sashes are of the same time.

Charles H. Dunham bought the property in two installments in 1863 and 1870. He lived in the Jones house until 1879 when he commissioned Charles H. Robinson to build the one next door: it was a tight fit on the lot. The town valuation list for 1880 assays the old house for $1,700 and the new one for $3,000, and on June 7th of that year Dunham disposed of the former for $700. His later residence is Eastlake in style, with a polygonal projection, complex window frames and eaves, pinnacles and crestings, and a bracketed cupola crowning the hip roof. This house was demolished in the late 1940s, but the brick building survives, looking much the same today as in the Wyer photograph here.

The Second Congregational Meetinghouse beyond was built by Elisha Ramsdell in 1809. It became Unitarian in 1824. The front pavilion with tower is a replacement, constructed by Perez Jenkins in 1830. The unusual shape may have come from Asher Benjamin's Charles Street Meetinghouse in West Boston, the plan and front elevation of which were delineated in the enlarged edition of Benjamin's *American Builder's Companion* of 1811. Nantucket's provincial version contains the town clock, an octagonal belfry for its famed Portuguese bell, and lookout for the town watch. capped by a gilt bonnet. The church was remodeled by Frederick Brown Coleman in 1844: the balcony was removed, the graceful vestibule stairs and low dome and apse in the auditorium were installed, and the interior was decorated by Carl Wendte. The metonym for the building is South Tower.

Above: **Plate 66. Philip's Block and Levi Starbuck House, Orange Street, late 19th c.** (Photograph by Henry S. Wyer, Nantucket Historical Association Collection). Philip H. Folger built five contiguous houses up the hill from his own residence at Main Street (Plate 46), also in 1831. The houses are duplexes, combining steps and doorways in pairs. They are the only row residences in the town, and their third stories are lighted by dormer windows, which are unique to ante-belleum domestic buildings here. Glass in transoms and sidelights is set directly in doorway members (rather than in separate frames) which is a common Nantucket practice. A plat survey in the town records, dated 16 January 1832, is inscribed with the names of the purchasers of the five new buildings in "Philip's Block." Kitchens were originally in

the basements, but today they are on the first floor of rear additions.

The second building from the right edge of the photograph is the most masculine residence in Nantucket, the Levi Starbuck House. The building faces south, and is made rigidly three-bayed by ponderous square piers on those sides visible from the street. Parapets crown the facade and portico, and these and other members are decorated with fretwork. Bold window frames cast shadows on the smooth, flush-board walls. The middle windows at both levels on the Orange Street flank are blind, and they are unprecedented in having glazed sashes outside closed paneled shutters, rather than the usual fixed louvered shutters. A handsome spiked fence with tall pedestal posts frames the yard. The interior space is regulated

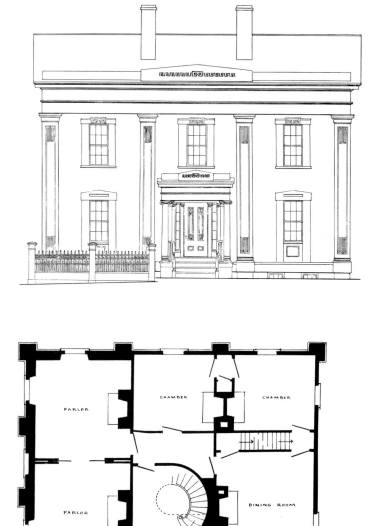

by the openings and by four evenly-spaced chimneys, yet it achieves variety and distinction, its curved staircase being unusually graceful. The parlors are embellished with elaborate plasterwork, with grape and acanthus motifs, and painted wall panels. The builder was William M. Andrews, who purchased the lot for $1,850 in August, 1836. His design here is more formal and advanced than that of his recently finished house on Hussey Street (Plate 78). Andrews sold "the new dwelling house" on Orange Street to Levi Starbuck for $5,000 in March 1838.

Right, top and bottom: **Plate 66A and 66B. Facade Elevation and First Floor Plan, Levi Starbuck House.**

## Bay View House.

This house from its commanding position and homelike appointments has become widely and favorably known as a favorite family resort. The house is open and all in order. The undersigned would be pleased to see all his former guests and the travelling public.

je21                                    J. PATTERSON.

Above: **Plate 67. Sherburne House, Orange Street, late 19th c.** (Photograph by Henry S. Wyer, Nantucket Historical Association Collection). The building on Orange Street about opposite Martin's Lane has been a caravansary for about half of its existence. It was built in 1831 by John B. Nicholson and served as the third Mansion House, under the proprietorship of Mrs. R. F. Parker for nine months after the Great Fire of 1846. Later owned by Zenas Adams, it became the Adams House in 1865, when John Winn began conducting it as a boardinghouse. John W. Macy bought the building for $6,000 in 1873 and changed its title to the Sherburne House. But Winn held the mortgage on the property and technically remained the owner. In 1877 the Sherburne was leased to the Mowry brothers, realtors and managers of the Springfield House (Plate 95), and in 1879, under the direction of manager Thomas H. Soule, a new period of prosperity was launched for the Sherburne. The building had attained the form shown, and a house across the street was leased as an annex. Extensive changes were made in 1891, but they were mostly at the back, including enlargement of the dining room. Up to the twentieth century the Sherburne was the foremost hostelry on Orange Street. In 1902 it was purchased by William Barnes, who had the main part of the structure stripped and moved back from the street. With rear additions, it was clothed in Colonial Revival dress and became the residence at No. 30. The house at the right in the photograph now stands opposite, at the south corner of Martin's Lane.

Above: **Plate 68. The Bay View House, 38 Orange Street, Rear View, late 19th c.** (Nantucket Historical Association Collection). The fine Greek Revival homestead of Frederick Gardner was built on Orange Street at Gorham's Court in the late 1830s. Freeman E. Adams acquired it in 1856, and in June 1873, after having made "extensive additions to his house during the past winter . . . he opened it for the reception of steady and transient boarders" according to the *Inquirer and Mirror*. The additions were the two-story ell at the rear and dormer windows on the roof for guest rooms in the garret. The public was advised that "The table will always be supplied with the best the market affords, and no pains will be spared to insure the comforts of its patrons." In April 1874 Adams' announcement in the newspaper was headed by the inn's new title, the "Bay View House." It had been suggested by the "high and central location, [which] commands a

pleasant view of the island, the harbor and the ocean." The vista undoubtedly soon attracted many guests, including the landscape painter, W. Henry Willard, who was a guest in the summer of 1876 when he invited the editor of the *Inquirer and Mirror* in to see his work. During the next few years, Adams turned over the management of the Bay View House to John W. Macy, of the Sherburne House. Afterwards, both hostelries were conducted by the Mowry brothers, and during most of the 1880s they were run by James Patterson. Guests are seen on the upper deck of the rear porch enjoying the harbor view. Today the back wing has been removed, the rear dormers are boxed together, and the porch has been altered.

Opposite, bottom: **Plate 68A. Sketch of the Bay View House** (From the *Inquirer and Mirror*, 21 June 1884, Atheneum Collection).

Above: **Plate 69. The Old Pump on Orange Street at Beaver Lane, late 1860s** (Nantucket Historical Association Collection). During the spring of 1804 the house on the far corner (second from the left) was built for David Wyer, mariner. At the end of the nineteenth century its doorway was furnished with an elaborate hood and the chimney was reduced to a small shaft. The house on the near corner. (left) was built by Richard Lake Coleman, housewright, and sold in February of 1807 to Capt. Jonathon Swain II for $1,000. Although Swain unloaded it at a loss ($930) to Joseph Killey in 1811, he was able to make money on other speculations in the neighborhood. The doorway and windows had been modernized when this photograph was made. The pump disappeared after the Wannacomet Water Company laid pipes down Orange Street during the early 1880s.

Orange Street was and remains the chief route in and out of Nantucket Town, giving access to points on the Great Harbor, the east end of the island, Siasconset and the south shore. The area below the Fish Lots was laid out as West Monomoy in 1726, and was known as Newtown at the beginning of the nineteenth century. The Newtown Gate, a barrier for excluding sheep near the first milestone on the Siasconset road, was in use up to 1840. Beaver Lane was laid out in 1760 between West Monomoy shares Nos. 8 and 9.

Opposite, top: **Plate 70. Isaiah Nicholson House, Fish Lane, Now 5 Spring Street, late 19th c.** (Photograph by Henry S. Wyer, Nantucket Historical Association Collection). Peter Russell's old lean-to house (extreme right) was the only building on Fish Lane when Isaiah Nicholson bought the large lot (forty-five and fifty-nine-hundredths rods) west of it in July 1833, and built what may be the last saltbox on Nantucket. Many of the later lean-tos were less than two full stories in front and had upstairs windows only on the ends, and those dating after 1750 had straight stairways at the back rather than winder steps in front of the chimney. Pegged frames persist around the windows, but the doorway has a suggestion of Classic elegance in its pilastered treatment, and the facade has been refined by the use of clapboards. The house is small, and its vestibule is but a step off the muddy lane. Nicholson sold it and a fourth of the land in November 1834 for $770. Within the next two years the house changed hands a couple of times. John J. Gardner bought it in 1836 for $750 and his heirs sold it forty year later (no sales price given). The name of Fish Lane was changed to Spring Street about 1880. Today, the front of the Nicholson house has been shingled and the windows altered; the Russell house is gone.

Bottom: **Plate 71. Richard Lake Coleman House, 21 Union Street, late 19th c.** (Photograph by Henry S. Wyer, Nantucket Historical Association Collection). Union Street was excluded from the Fish Lot subdivision (1717), whose harborside limit reached only to the brink of Quanaty Bank. Lower Union Street corresponds with the east boundary of West Monomoy (1726) to the south; and when Union Street was extended northward below the Fish Lots, the base of Quanaty Bank was cut back so houses could be built on its west side. Richard Lake Coleman, housewright (Plate 69), built this typical Nantucket house type (center) with gambrel roof on land purchased for $440 in the spring of 1796. Coleman erected a similar house, but with a simple pitched roof, three doors northward about 1800 (the side of the house is visible at the far left). These buildings have unusually high basements for the period, because of the slope of the land. In 1803 Coleman sold 21 Union Street to William Nichols for $2,000, the property including a "dwelling house, shop, barn and other out buildings." Nichols also was a housewright, and undoubtedly would have made good use of all the structures. The two houses shown at the left were removed in 1902, with the sale of the Sherburne House lot to William Barnes (Plate 67). When Wyer made the photograph the windows of the Coleman house had been given larger and fewer panes. In 1970 twelve-over-twelve and nine-over-nine-paned sashes were restored.

Above: **Plate 72. Methodist Episcopal Church, Centre at Liberty Street, late 19th c.** (Stereograph by Josiah Freeman, Nantucket Historical Association Collection). This corner is on the south boundary of the Wesco Acre Lots, laid out in 1678. A dwelling was built here in 1733 for Richard Mitchell, whose son, Peleg Mitchell, sold the land to Dr. Oliver L. Bartlett for $4,680 in 1822. Mitchell reserved the right to remove the house and all building materials. In the fall of 1823 the trustees of the Methodist Episcopal Church, a separatist group from the "Teaser" meeting on Fair Street, paid Dr. Bartlett $4,000 for the property, and at that time their chapel was standing. It was a nearly-square, hip-roofed frame building, containing an auditorium with balcony, which could seat one thousand persons, and it cost $14,000 to build. The chapel was dedicated by the Rev. John Newland Moffitt and others on September 24th. In 1840 the building was given a new look when Frederick Brown Coleman added the monumental Ionic portico, including a pediment at the front, a ridge roof with gable at the rear and a full entablature along the flanks supported by pilasters at the extremities. An appropriate spike fence with rails and square posts enclosed the front yard. From this time on the building ceased to be called the chapel and was known as the Methodist Episcopal Church. A hedge now replaces the fence.

Opposite, top: **Plate 73. Centre Street, from the Main-Liberty Intersection, 1870s–80s** (Stereograph by Josiah Freeman, Nantucket Historical Association Collection). The west flank of the Union Block (right), which fronts Main Street, facing Orange, is articulated by a series of tall recessed panels, pierced by windows and divided by a cornice between the first and second floors, and crowned by a pediment. Walls are of brick, cornices of brownstone, and the roof is slate. The second building from the right is the No. 8 Engine Company, whose thick fire pole stands at the curb. Beyond, Sherburne Hall (here barely glimpsed through the trees) is a handsome Greek Revival composition of five pavilions housing six shops at street level and a spacious hall above. The building was commissioned by Benjamin F. Riddell and James Athearn after its predecessors burned in the Great Fire of 1846. Constructed entirely of wood, the new edifice was ready for occupancy within five months. Originally referred to as the Centre Street Block, the name soon was established in its present form, prompting Charles B. L'Hommedieu to call his candy and ice-cream emporium here the Sherburne Saloon. When another tenant, Andrew M. Macy, joined the Gold Rush to California toward the end of 1848, his bookstore was taken over by his sister, Harriet, who was the first of many distaff shopkeepers, causing the stretch to be called "Petticoat Row." The great upper hall in the building was used briefly as S. A. C. Flu's dancing school, before becoming the permanent headquarters of the Independent Order of Odd Fellows, who now share the hall with the Daughters of Rebekah.

Opposite, bottom: **Plate 73A. Restored Front Elevation, Sherburne Hall.**

Above: **Plate 74. Roberts House, Northeast Corner of Centre and India Streets, late 19th c.** (Stereograph by Platt Brothers, Nantucket Historical Association Collection). The elderly Elizabeth H. Mitchell deeded her home at the northeast corner of Centre and Pearl (India) Streets to Dr. David G. Hussey in 1873, for the considerations of semiannual payments of $600 and her support for the remainder of her life. In the mid-1880s the building became Mrs. Austin's boardinghouse. At the auction sale in the spring of 1896 it was purchased by John Roberts and was operated by him as the Roberts House. The building contained three parlors and seventeen lodging rooms. An extension was built to the side of the distyle portico (enlarged into a full piazza in 1902), and, at street level, railings (shown in the photograph) were set up to either side of the slabs over the gutter at the corner. Adjoining the Roberts House on Centre Street was the New Bedford Monthly Meetinghouse, built by the Friends in the mid-nineteenth century. In 1899 the meetinghouse became a Baptist Church and in 1911 it was annexed to the Roberts House as a dining hall. The last of John Roberts' three daughters, Mary E., sold the building in 1959 when she was 84 years of age and no longer able to run the establishment by herself. It continued for a while

as the Bayberry Inn, and in 1975 it resumed its old title. The restaurant is now called the Meeting House.

Opposite: **Plate 75. Southwest Corner of Centre and India Streets, late 1860s** (Nantucket Historical Association Collection). Avis Pinkham lost not only his house to the Great Fire of 1846 but a rod of land afterward when Centre and Pearl (now India) Streets were widened. For the loss of the land he was compensated $199 by the town. On the remaining trapezoid-shaped lot Pinkham built the Greek Revival clapboarded house shown. His residence has a four-bayed facade, pilasters in the doorway and at the corners of the building, and is capped by a pediment with fan window in front and a paneled parapet on the flanks. Pinkham mortgaged his property to the Nantucket Institution for Savings for $1,000 in March 1847, and the bank foreclosed in February 1861. Judging by the costumes of the people shown, the photograph must have been taken later in the decade. The pose of the little girl and brothers holding hands are mid-Victorian attitudes. Primitive landscape paintings are shown set in the downstairs windows. The culvert at the lower right-hand corner solicited the protective fence sections shown in Plate 74. The building is now used commerically and is spoiled by a shop front.

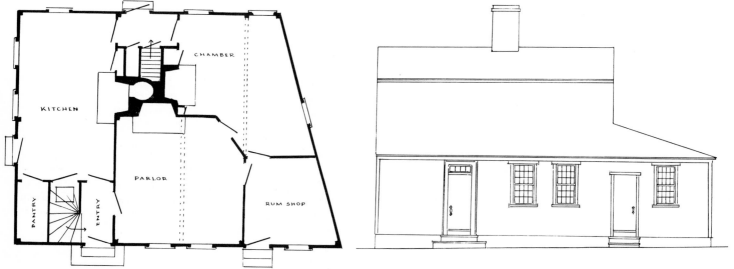

Opposite, top: **Plate 76. West End of Pearl Street, Now India Street, 1881** (Stereograph by Josiah Freeman, Nantucket Historical Association Collection). Joseph Sansom had said in the January 1811 issue of the *Port Folio* (Plate 2A) that the stretch of Pearl Street shown in this photograph was called "India Row" because of the "number of residents who lived in ease and affluence thereon," a remark which influenced the change of the street's name a century later. Nevertheless, the east end persisted as "Lower Pearl" into the 1960s. Except for the big white house with four chimneys, midway up the block on the left, all of the buildings pictured were standing at the time of Sansom's statement. Beyond the first two with center halls on the right, the four-bayed typical Nantucket house-type prevails on the north side of the street. The first dwelling opposite, on the left, was erected for Silas Paddock in 1767. Its odd angles, both outside and inside, and its clustering of fireplaces, cupboards and closets, its steep stairways (one by the chimney), and the addendum of a little rum shop on the far end make it one of the most picturesque buildings on the island. When this photograph was made in 1881 Pearl Street's cobblestone paving was exposed.

Opposite, bottom: **Plate 76A. First Floor Plan and Front Elevation, Silas Paddock House.**

Above: **Plate 77. The Gardner Houses, Bunker's Court, Now Part of Hussey Street, late 19th c.** (Photograph by Henry S. Wyer, Anonymous Private Collection). Hussey Street was a dead-end way known as Hussey Court at the beginning of the nineteenth century. A lane curving up from Liberty Street, called Bunker's Court, was later continued to make the present Hussey Street. Bunker's Court served the narrow spur of Academy Hill that formed the west boundary of the Wesco Acre Lots. Academy Hill was originally granted to Richard Gardner, and his descendants built houses there. The east side of the large house behind the wagon in the photograph was the lean-to residence of Caleb Gardner (Richard's great-grandson), erected in 1735. Its chimney (barely visible) is composed of three withes. The west end of the house (left) has smaller windows in the second story and a one-story extension covered by a shed roof on the end. The gambrel-roofed house to the right was built in 1772 for Grafton Gardner, the grandson of Richard's brother, John. John had married Priscilla Grafton, whose maiden name descended to their grandson. The railings capping both the open-slat and closed-planked sections of the fence are typical in Nantucket. The sidewalk in front of the fence is rustically conceived.

Above: **Plate 78. West End of Old Hussey Court, late 19th c.**
(Photograph by Henry S. Wyer, Nantucket Historical Association
Collection). At the right of the photograph is the side of the Caleb
Gardner house, whose front is featured in Plate 77. Of prime
interest here is the second house up the street. It was built by
William M. Andrews, who was a few days short of twenty-three
years of age in the summer of 1834, when he bought the north half
of Lydia Bunker's homestead (facing India Street) for $265.32.
Andrews must have had construction under way in the spring of
1836, at which time he took out an $800 mortgage on the property.
The building was finished on December 13th when it was sold to
Henry Parkinson for $1,800. Andrews lavished the best archi-
tectural dress he knew on the house (Plate 78A); there are slender
fluted pilasters flanking the doorway and at each end of the
facade, connected by entablatures, the principal one encircling the
house, and the doorway has sidelights and a paneled frieze in lieu
of a transom. The steep pediment crowning the facade has a tym-
panum with a wheel window set in a triangle. Muntins radiating
from the corners of the glass are connected by curved dividers
between the panes, and the effect is that of a great spider's web.
The point that Andrews missed in the design is the lack of Classic
base, as the house sits close to the ground. This shortcoming and
any other weaknesses it may have were corrected in the builder's
next bold undertaking (Plate 66A). The neighboring home of Louis
B. Imbert (with pediment to the right) bears a resemblance to the
Parkinson residence, having corresponding elements, though the
window in the pediment was a depressed lunette. The Imbert house
was built shortly before and may have set the precedent for
Andrew's undertaking. Its lunette has been replaced by a rectangular window.
Right: **Plate 78A. Front Elevation, Henry Parkinson
House.**

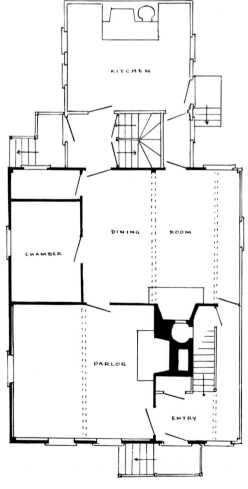

Above: **Plate 79. William Brock House, Centre at Quince Street, late 19th c.** (Photograph by Henry S. Wyer, Nantucket Historical Association Collection). Ebenezer Calef had built a barn on this lot when he paid Peter Jenkins £69/6/- for it in 1767. The barn was the only structure standing here when Calef's orphaned (and widowed) daughter, Elizabth Brock, sold a share of it to her son, William, for £40 in 1788. William and his mother commissioned a two-story residence having a "half-house" plan, with winder stairs in front of the chimney. Mother Brock occupied two rooms upstairs, known as the "Front Chamber" and the "Southern Bed Chamber," both on the street side of the house. The arrangement was recorded by deed on 18 March 1800, the day before William sold his part of the property to Thomas Brock II for $850. In the Nantucket tradition, Elizabeth Brock was to retain the two rooms exclusively, with use of "the Garrett and Cellar and a priviledge [sic] to pass in and out at all times" for her lifetime. In all probability it was for her comfort, and Thomas' need for more room, that a three-foot strip on the north side of the existing house and a two-story service ell at the rear were added. The wedge-shaped steps to a small entry were replaced by a straight flight to a hall, the old kitchen became a dining room (the former oven a closet under the stairs), and a respectable back stairway was included in the ell. The archaic "half-house" had been transformed into an up-to-date "typical." From 1895 to 1912 this was the Pitman (boarding) House, and it sported a gingerbread porch across the front. The porch has been removed, and the house serves today as the main pavilion of a gift shop.

Left: **Plate 79A. First Floor Plan, William Brock House, with Additions.**

Above: **Plate 80. Nathan Coffin House, 14 Quince Street, before 1877** (Photograph by Henry S. Wyer, Nantucket Historical Association Collection). The site of the old lean-to house shown is toward the west end of Crown Court, the old name for the street that begins alongside the William Brock residence, now called Quince Street. It is in the second squadron of the Wesco Acre Lots laid out in 1678, which was reapportioned in 1720 when the piece of ground considered here went to James Coffin II. Six years later James bestowed it on his son, Nathan Coffin, who presumably built the house shortly thereafter. It seems odd that the house should have its rear toward the preexisting lane, but such were the dictates of early orientation. The dwelling was in the Coffin family until purchased at auction for $335 by Samuel H. Winslow in 1851. Winslow's heirs sold it to Asa T. Pierce for $475 in 1887, and Pierce enlarged it for use as a summer home. The new street front became two-storied and featured a projecting bay window, with a gingerbread porch at the northeast corner. Today the late-Victorian details have been stripped off and the walls shingled to give an old appearance.

Opposite, top left: **Plate 80A. Restored First Floor Plan, Nathan Coffin House.**

Opposite, top right: **Plate 80B. The Coffin House, as Enlarged by Asa T. Pierce, after 1887.**

Opposite, bottom: **Plate 81. The Tallant School and Fair Street Academy, late 1860s** (Stereograph by Josiah Freeman, Nantucket Historical Association Collection). At the mid-mark of the nineteenth century Nantucket had three large grammar schools—the North, the South and the West—besides the Bear Street Primary and a primary school on York Street for Black children. Soon the town acquired the new Coffin School on Winter Street and the High School on Westminster Street (Academy Hill). Caroline L. Tallant and her sister, Maria, were conducting a private school on Federal Street in Harmony Hall, formerly the Sons of Temperance meeting place and later the Catholic Church (predecessor of the present building). The Misses Tallant moved to the little Greek Revival building on Fair Street at the south corner of Charter Street. But when Freeman took his picture this may have been the Fair Street Academy of Hepsibeth Hussey, who formerly taught at the Friends School northward at the intersection of Ray's Court. She gave up the Academy in 1871. In the southwest view from South Tower (Plate 41) the schoolhouse is seen on its original site to the left. It subsequently was moved to its present location at 8 Quince Street, where it serves as a private home.

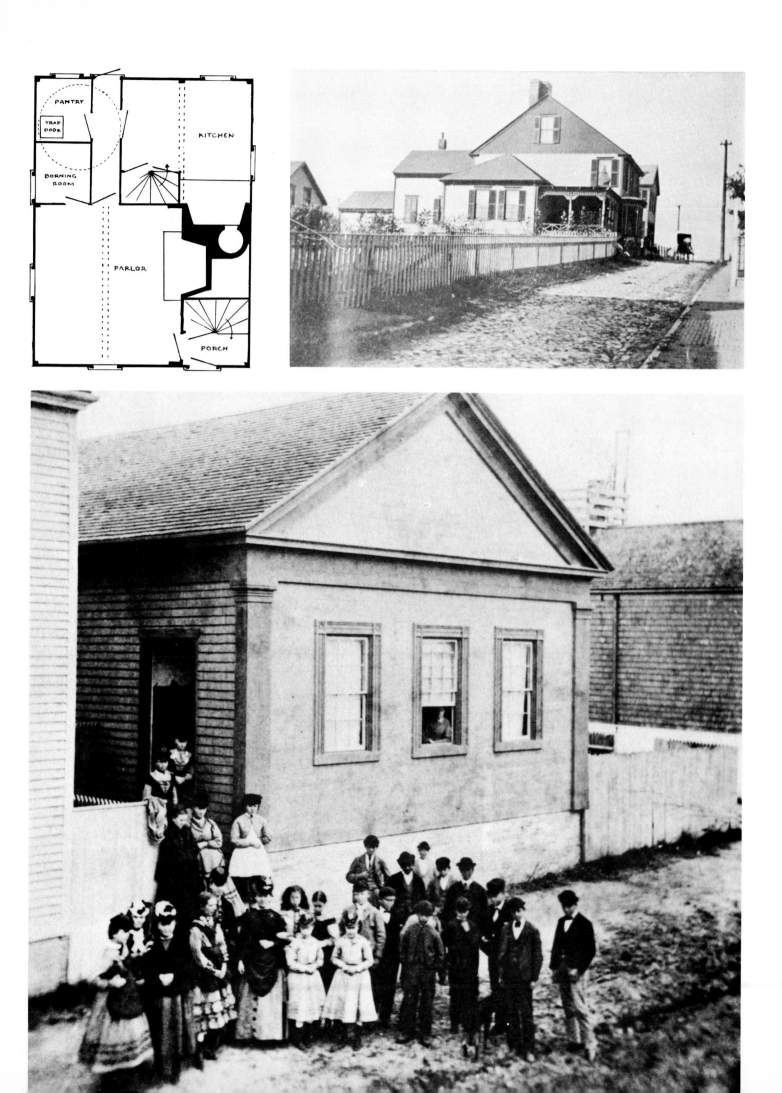

Above: **Plate 82. Looking East from the Summit of Gay Street, late 19th c.** (Photograph by Henry S. Wyer, Nantucket Historical Association Collection). Gay Street originally was called Coffin Court, after Joshua Coffin, a bit of whose house (1756) may be seen at the lower end, partly concealing the Ocean (Jared Coffin) House beyond. The Atlantic Silk Company was established in the building on the extreme right, built during 1835–36, and the name of the street was changed to honor Gameliel Gay, the mechanic-inventor who installed steam-powered machinery in the mill. To feed the silkworms, mulberry trees were planted behind the George Easton house on North Water Street. After eight years, however, the silk industry failed on Nantucket. Samuel B. Tuck, one of the prime investors, reclaimed a portion of his losses through constructing and selling the small Greek Revival houses on the left side of the street. The factory building itself was converted into a duplex. In 1872 the east half (right, behind the tree) began to be operated as William A. Searell's Waverly House; three years later the piazza was built. During the 1890s it was the Summit, run in conjunction with a new adjoining guesthouse, called the Hillside. The combination continued through the first quarter of the twentieth century. The Hillside and the porch shown on the Summit are gone, but the latter building continues to accommodate visitors.

Opposite, top: **Plate 83. The Ocean House, Broad at Centre Street, ca. 1871** (Stereograph by Josiah Freeman, Nantucket Historical Association Collection). On this corner, the most enduring inn site in Nantucket, stood Paul Gardner's frame residence, which became J. A. Parker's boardinghouse in 1831, and John Thornton's Mansion House five years later. Jared Coffin bought and razed that building, and he built the present brick residence in 1845 to appease a wife bored with living at Moor's End, on the edge of town (Plate 41). Mrs. Coffin soon found the downtown house no more to her liking, and Jared took her to Boston. The briefly-occupied building was purchased in the spring of 1847 by the Nantucket Steamboat Company and opened as a hotel called the Ocean House. Freeman's picture must have been taken no later than 1871, as it seems to have served as the model for an engraving accompanying an advertisement offering the hostelry for sale in January of the following year (Plate 83 A). The artisan of the print took the expected liberties of opening the shutters, eliminating most of the animate litter except for the one-horse buggy on the right and the two figures on the portico. The

American flag, blurred in the photograph, is brought out clearly on the print.

The Ocean House was purchased in November 1872 by Allen L. Howe and William A. Elmer of Boston, who appointed George W. Macy proprietor, and it was Macy who had the honor of entertaining the first incumbent President of the United States to come to the island. On 27 August 1874 Ulysses S. and Mrs. Grant made a two-hour visit. They were driven through the principal streets of the town and taken to the Ocean House to dine. For that occasion the front of the building was hung with red, white and blue streamers from eaves to balcony, and a portrait of the President was centered over the flag-and-flower-festooned portico. The Head of State enjoyed his brief sojourn at the dinner table and dispatched the postmaster general to greet the townspeople thronging the street on his behalf. A better show than a speech was provided when the Grants took their places in the carriage for the ride back to the boat. A rein became entangled, and the horses bolted. The First Lady got out and walked, but the General kept his seat for the three-block ride.

Right: **Plate 83A. The Ocean House** (From the *Inquirer and Mirror*, 13 January 1872, Atheneum Collection).

Opposite, top: **Plate 84. Peter Folger II House, 51 Centre Street, late 19th c.** (Photograph by Henry S. Wyer, Nantucket Historical Association Collection). The date of the old three-storied "flat-roofed house" on Centre Street is furnished by a receipt of 3 November 1765, from Jethro Hussey, housewright, to Peter Folger II for "28 pounds, 10 shillings on account of building his house;" and when Folger sold it to John Elkins for 150 pounds on 23 March 1792, he referred to it as "my Dwelling House . . . built in the year one Thousand Seven hundred and Sixty-five." The building stands on the site of the William Gayer dwelling of 1683, which was moved to and incorporated into No. 3 Step Lane, seen at the right of the photograph. The "flat-roofed house" took its name from the roof deck whose boards were coated with tar, covered with paper and a thin layer of cement, the whole surrounded by a railing. There must have been leakage, for early in the nineteenth century a pitched roof was added, the old deck remaining as the garret floor. Other alterations of the same time consisted of adding a kitchen ell on the north side and an entrance pent in front, exchanging the old winder stairway for a straight flight in a crosswise hall, converting the two rooms on the south side to parlors and combining part of the former parlor with a back hall to form a new dining room opposite, convenient to the kitchen addition. The house is unique in Nantucket in retaining its eighteenth-century beaded-edge clapboards affixed with rose-headed nails. Peter Folger II kept and handed down the east or lower side of the land (on North Water Street). His grandson and namesake acquired the homestead on Centre Street at auction in 1852. The house then remained in the family until 1955.

Opposite, bottom left: **Plate 84A. Original First Floor Plan, "Flat-roofed House" (bottom); After additions (top).**

Opposite, bottom right: **Plate 84B. Restored Front Elevation, "Flat-roofed House."**

Above: **Plate 85. Old North Vestry, Academy Hill, late 19th c.** (Photograph by Henry S. Wyer, Nantucket Historical Association). The oldest structure used for worship on Nantucket, this building was originally the Presbyterian North Shore Meetinghouse, erected shortly before the summer of 1732. In the same year the Peter Folger II house was being built across the street, (1765), the framework of the meetinghouse was brought to Academy Hill and reassembled for the Congregational Society. The "inside work" of the structure was stored in the old Town House at Main and Milk streets pending installation the following summer. A square tower was added on the south front and may be glimpsed in the Thomas Birch view of the town (Plate 2). In 1834 the building (without the tower) was moved westward from the crest of the hill, and it became the North Vestry. Supporting members are plainly visible inside, although the early upper gallery is missing. Today it is surrounded by additions on all four sides. Backing up its east flank in the photograph is the First Congregational Church proper, the cause of the last site-change of the North Vestry. The somewhat Classic, somewhat Gothic church was built by Samuel Waldron of Boston, and about 1840 the auditorium was lengthened one bay and the top of the tower removed. When the church was restored in 1968 a new steeple was built on the ground and hoisted by helicopter. The church is also known by the name of North Tower.

Left: **Plate 86. Portico, Reuben R. Bunker House, Academy Hill, ca. 1900** (Nantucket Historical Association Collection). The house behind the First Congregational Church on Academy Hill was built on land Reuben R. Bunker procured in 1806 from the heirs of Caleb Macy. The residence was a plain Quaker type, square and two-storied, with irregularly spaced openings and shingled walls. About 1820 a transformation took place, whereby the house was enlarged and given Classic elegance. A one-bay addition on the west side put the front door at the middle opening, in count if not in spacing, and it was sheltered by a charming little colonnetted portico, with a small vault bridging two flank entablatures. Clapboards replaced the shingles on the walls, and wooden quoins stabilized the extremities. The house remained in the family ninety years, passing through the hands of several children to a granddaughter, Sara Bunker, who, as a "femme sole," sold it to Susan H. Palmer in 1887. The purity of the Classic portico is marred in the photograph by later railings and benches.

Above: **Plate 86A. Front Elevation, Reuben R. Bunker House, Remodeled and Enlarged.**

Above: **Plate 87. Robinson and Chadwick Cottages, 70–72 Centre Street, late 19th c.** (Photograph by Henry S. Wyer, Nantucket Historical Association Collection). In June 1838 Susanne Wyer sold adjoining lots below the new First Congregational Church to Isaiah H. Robinson and John Chadwick, both housewrights. (Chadwick was to be the builder of the Baptist Church, shown in Plate 60.) Each lot fronted one and eighty-two hundredths rods (about thirty feet) on Centre Street and cost $300, and the following spring each was mortgaged to William Keen for $600, an indication that improvements had been made. At the beginning of 1841 Chadwick and Robinson signed an agreement to keep a nine-and-one-half-foot carriageway between the houses perpetually open. On April 3rd Chadwick sold the near house to George Harris for $1,500, and on the same day paid off his mortgage to Keen; Robinson did not satisfy his loan until November 1865.

The two cottages are identical. They are Greek Revival in style, with clapboarded walls, pilasters at the corners and deep entablatures on the flanks. The buildings are less than two full stories, and the break in the entablature in front and back allows for upper fenestration. The outer windows with quarter-round tops make for an interesting shutter pattern. Stoop railings tie in with the front fences, integrating the architecture with the street. Note parapet balustrades over the cornices on the flanks, lately removed from the buildings. There are about a dozen other residences following these models in Nantucket.

Left: **Plate 87A. Front Elevation, John Chadwick Cottage.**

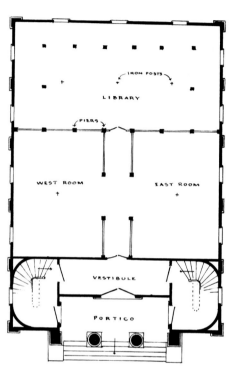

Opposite, top: **Plate 88. Swain's Boardinghouse, Centre at Lily Street, 1870s** (Stereograph by Josiah Freeman, Nantucket Historical Association Collection). Staff and guests are gathered in front of the boardinghouse at the north corner of Centre and Lily Streets. During the 1870s the house was owned by J. B. Swain and run by Samuel Davis, and then later by James B. Coffin, who called it the Brattleboro House. In 1895 Calvert Handy, a former restaurateur on Steamboat Wharf, took over and named the establishment the Central House. The following year he kept it open all winter. At the end of the century Handy assumed management of the Waverly House on Gay Street (Plate 82), and Thurston C. Swain became the owner and proprietor of the Central House. The popular name for it throughout its life as an inn has been Swain's Boardinghouse.

Opposite, bottom: **Plate 89. Seth Ray House, North Liberty Street, late 19th c.** (Photograph by Henry S. Wyer, Nantucket Historical Association Collection). One of the most singular houses in Nantucket is that built by Seth Ray on land for which he paid Eliphulet Paddock $30 on 25 June 1798. The spot is west of the Lily Pond and was identified as being part of Crooked Record. Seth Ray already had enclosed it with a fence, and he evidently set to work immediately building his home. He took out a mortgage for $450 on November 13th of that year, and the property was described as containing a dwelling-house. The building belongs to three distinct categories of Nantucket architecture: it is a gambrel-roof house; because of the extension at the rear, it is also a lean-to; and its facade and room arrangement make it a typical Quaker-type. The interior has undergone changes, especially about the fireplaces, but the outside appears little different today.

Above, left: **Plate 90. Nantucket Atheneum, India at Federal Street, ca. 1870** (Stereograph by Josiah Freeman, Nantucket Historical Association Collection). The handsomest building in Nantucket is the Atheneum, designed by Frederick Brown Coleman (Plates 49 and 60) and built by Charles Wood during the winter of 1846–47. It is constructed of wood, the outer walls composed of boards set flush to one another, with colossal pilastrades and two tiers of windows on the flanks, and a double-pedimented facade unmarred by fenestration on the south side. In the recessed portico are beautifully modeled Greek Ionic columns *in antis*, and a great pilastered doorway. The front yard is framed by a railing fence of sufficient visual stability to complement the architecture. The edifice was erected on the foundations of the old Atheneum that burned in the Great Fire of 1846 (Plate 25), and is larger than its predecessor in that it has stairways enclosed within the area of the old portico. Behind the portico the first story has a vestibule that extends to the back wall of the stairway sections. The great space behind is divided by rows of square piers, some having screen walls connecting them, and a few slender iron posts supplement the piers in supporting the floor above. In the second story is an auditorium claiming a seating capacity of six hundred. The upper space has a stage at the north end and coved ceiling above. The Nantucket Atheneum was opened on 1 February 1847. In 1900 it became a free public library. A children's section was installed in the basement in 1963, and a conference room and vault were included in a new east wing added in 1966.

Above, right: **Plate 90A. Restored First Floor Plan, Nantucket Atheneum.**

Opposite, top: **Plate 91. The Atheneum Museum, late 1890s** (Photograph by Platt Bros., Nantucket Historical Association Collection). Besides serving as a library, the Atheneum was used for meetings, lectures, exhibitions and entertainments—and even for a murder trial. Most of the extra-curricular activities were held in the upstairs auditorium. The downstairs housed the museum's books and artifacts. The old Atheneum's museum collection had been wiped out by the Great Fire of 1846. Some books out on loan were saved, however, and these formed the nucleus of the new collection. Art objects and curios were acquired slowly, and in conjunction with the Atheneum Fair of 1870 an exhibition of portraits was held. By the end of the decade the collection had become sufficiently ample to warrant permanent display. The "hundreds of strange things . . . collected from nearly every part of the globe," as the *Inquirer and Mirror* described them, were scattered among the book shelves in the big north room and given exclusive sanctuary forward. Featured was the "monster *Sperm Whale's Jaw,* seventeen feet long, in perfect condition, with all the teeth in place." There was also a model of the "Camels" (Plate 91A), a trough-shaped device used on Nantucket for hauling large vessels through the channel into the harbor before the jetties were built. A whaler in proper scale was included in the model. Explanations of the "wonders" were given to visitors by Joseph S. Swain. Joe (shown here fondling the whale's jaw) was available to "Parties desirous of entrance in evenings." The entrance fee at any time was 15¢. The Atheneum's museum collection now has been mostly divided between the Peter Folger and Whaling Museum.

Opposite, bottom: **Plate 91A. Model of the "Camels," early 1870s** (Stereograph by Josiah Freeman, Nantucket Historical Association).

Above: **Plate 92. Broad Street, Looking West from Water Street, late 19th c.** (Photograph by Henry S. Wyer, Nantucket Historical Association Collection). Hidden under the cobblestones in the foregound is a cistern that was installed in 1832. It failed, though, to placate the destructive fire of 13 July 1846, that destroyed all buildings on the street with the exception of Jared Coffin's house, at the far end (Plate 83). In 1847, when the Coffin residence became the Ocean House and the wharf was converted to a steamboat landing, Broad Street became the reception center of Nantucket. The first house on the right was, from 1895 onward, the boardinghouse of the artist George G. Fish and his wife (Plate 29). The second house, built for William T. Swain, after 1876, also served as a boardinghouse after it passed to Charlotte W. Pettee (proprietor of the Sea Cliff Inn, see Plate 120) in 1888, and to John D. Nesbitt in 1895. This and the next building (now the Nesbitt Inn) were managed together. The two-story Greek Revival building on a high basement and with pediment was Mrs. G. W. Hooper's hostelry, called The Gables, at the turn of the century. Beyond it is a small office building. Set back in the yard between the Gables and the Ocean House is the Eben Allen cottage (Plate 27).

Broad Street, only a few short blocks from Main, was originally the upper boundary of the east range of Wesco Acre Lots (1678) and of the Bocochico Shares (1744), and beyond it were the southeast homesites of old Sherburne. At the end of the eighteenth century Isaac Coffin described Broad as extending from Centre "east to New North Wharf." Near Centre stood the Friends North Meetinghouse, converted in 1839 into the Episcopal Trinity Church (Plate 26). At that time the Mansion House occupied the corner.

Opposite: **Plate 93. North Water Street from Broad Street, 1870s–80s** (Stereograph by Josiah Freeman, Nantucket Historical Association Collection). The lot of the first house on the left, fronting thirty-six and one-half feet on North Water Street, was purchased by Edward F. Easton on 28 October 1845. If he built anything on it during the next eight months it would have been destroyed by the Great Fire of 1846. Easton was a housewright, and the residence he constructed for himself soon after that disaster achieved distinction by combining equal elements of Greek and Gothic Revival architecture (Plate 93A). The

first style is represented by the high podium, the peristyle of polygonal posts set on square plinths and the entablature all around. The second style is embodied in the steep roof and sharply pitched window heads set on colonnettes in the front gable. There is a simplicity, if not naivete, about this early eclecticism that limits each of the two styles to its own level. The rear ell of the Easton house juts out at an odd angle, following the bend in the lot. Today the sidewalk on the west side of North Water Street has been widened, and the frontal stairs to the doorway have been exchanged for steps running to the side of a stoop.

Left: **Plate 93A. Restored Front Elevation, Edward F. Easton House.**

Above: **Plate 94. William Whippey House, 3 Whaler's Lane, late 19th c.** (Photograph by Henry S. Wyer, Nantucket Historical Association Collection). Whaler's Lane, just north of Broad Street, connecting North Water with South Beach Street, remained nameless as late as 1870, when Eunice H. Whippey sold her home to a neighbor, Mark Solon. The residence built by her late husband, William Whippey, housewright, at mid-century is unusual in having a broad front that is only one-room deep on the east end (right of the house). The shallowness of the shape is accentuated by the high basement. Like the nearby Easton house the building mixes two styles: the facade has a Greek Doric portico, matching pilasters at the corners, and entablature on the flanks, and, over the entrance, a Gothicized window, with two corbel-arched lights and a quatrefoil inset at the top of the pointed framework. Electric wires dip in front of the gable of the house. At the extreme right may be seen the rear of the new Springfield House (Plate 97). Two signs on the sill at eye level announce "Rooms to Let." The portico already had been altered when, in 1973, the original clapboards were stripped off and replaced by unsophisticated shingles.

Above: **Plate 95. Elijah Alley's Hotel, Later Springfield House, North Water at Chester Street, ca. 1880** (Stereograph by Josiah Freeman, Nantucket Historical Association Collection). The trend to hostelries in the north end of town, which was nearer bathing facilities, started at the time of the Civil War. Elijah H. Alley purchased a large building at the corner of North Water and Chester Streets in 1863-64. Since 1836 it had been serving as two ample residences, and Alley added a full third story under a mansard roof. The dining room and kitchen were rele- gated to ground level, the parlors remained on the first floor, and twenty-five rooms were rented to guests. Alley eventually tired of the venture and tried to sell or lease the building in the spring of 1874. He had no success, so he had to manage it himself during the summer, but toward the close of the season Albert S. Mowry, who was running a small boardinghouse called the Springfield at what is now 21 North Water Street, leased the Alley house for several years. The little building across the street had been purchased by Albert's brother, Almon T. Mowry, in 1872, and the Mowrys had

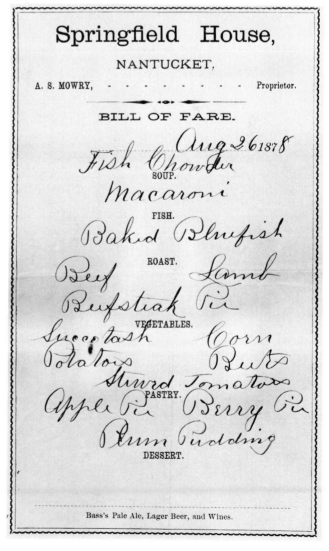

named it after their hometown in western Massachusetts. With the second building at their disposal, the brothers added an extension to the north side of the original Springfield to serve as a dining room for both sections. The old dining room in the basement of the Alley building became a billiard room.

In 1917, when its corner location was considered a traffic menace, the Town purchased the property for $3,500 and sold the building for $95 to be moved from the land. The street now cuts across part of its site.

Above: **Plate 96. The Springfield House and Annex, North Water Street, ca. 1880** (Photograph by Henry S. Wyer, Nantucket Historical Association Collection). In the spring of 1878 the *Inquirer and Mirror* announced: "The name of the Springfield House has been placed in the concrete walk in front of it in white marble mosaic—the first work of the kind ever done here." The letters, nine or ten inches high, are at the foot of the stairs to the right in the photograph. If any doubt lingered as to which was the main pavilion of the Springfield, the pavement label dispelled it.

In August 1878 Elijah H. Alley bought Nancy Fisher's house across the street, and, as on the building in Plate 95, added a third story within a mansard roof; "a spacious piazza" was built across the front. The Mowry brothers leased it as well, and when opened in 1879 it became the Annex House, later called Annex No. 1.

Right: **Plate 96A. The Springfield's Dinner Menu, 26 August 1878** (Nantucket Historical Association Collection).

Above: **Plate 97. The New Springfield, 19 North Water Street, after 1883** (Photograph by Henry S. Wyer, Nantucket Historical Association Collection). In 1880 Albert S. Mowry bought the large lot south of the original Springfield House that extended to south Beach Street. In 1883 James H. Gibbs constructed what at first was to be called the "New House," but which came to be the principal pavilion of the complex. The building was three full stories, though the different treatment of the top related it to the mansard roofs of the two buildings at the north end of the block. The new Springfield portion had a one-story porch across the front which at one time extended to the dining-hall building next door (extreme left). The parlor in the northwest corner was a noteworthy room. It was forty-five feet long and at the back had a mantel of painted panels hailed as "Morceaux in Art." Motifs included a seascape, an allegory of eventide (a female figure in diaphanous draperies), and island birds and flora, the work of William Ferdinand Macy, a descendant of Thomas Macy, the Nantucket First Purchaser. Macy was born at New Bedford in 1852, and according to his obituary, studied in New York under Robert Swain Gifford, "and [Joseph Oriel (?)] Eaton the portrait painter." The rest of the new building contained twenty-two sleep-

ing rooms, and water was piped to conveniences on each floor. Every room was provided with gas lighting fixtures and steam radiators, supplied by C. H. Mowry of Springfield, undoubtedly a relative. At the close of 1883 Albert S. Mowry gave a New Year's party for all of the artisans and mechanics who had a share in creating the "New Springfield." Enlarged and sadly altered, the original clapboards replaced by shingles, the building is now the Harbor House.

Opposite, top: **Plate 98. Veranda House, Step Lane at North Water Street** (From the *Inquirer and Mirror*, 17 May 1884, Atheneum Collection). Beginning in 1882 the Springfield had a nearby rival—the Veranda House. The nucleus of the building is said to be part of the William Gayer house of 1684, which faced Centre Street and was taken down to make way for the Peter Folger II residence of 1765 (Plate 84). The Veranda House was the home of Nathan Chapman, who began calling Step Lane "Chapman Avenue" when he started his boardinghouse; but which name was not generally accepted and did not persist. The hostel was described as being "located near the shore of the harbor on elevated ground, a short distance from the steam boat landing. . . . This house has been fitted with eighteen large, airy rooms, and

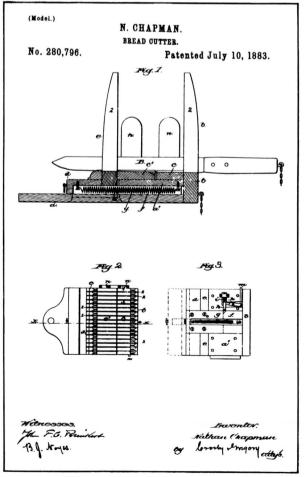

three spacious verandas on each of three sides of the house, where patrons may enjoy the benefit of the sea breezes." Rates were "$9.00 to $11.00 per week . . . $2.00 to $2.50 per day . . . Children under 10 years $4.00 to $7.00." In 1883 Chapman purchased the home of James B. Gibbs, the Springfield House contractor, at what is now 20 North Water Street, and connected the old building with the new annex. Another residence, known as the Joy house, was standing on the corner, and Chapman had it moved to the south side of Step Lane. Its former site was terraced and served as a recreation ground for guests. The fully developed establishment is shown here in the engraving. In 1890 a wing was added to the north side of the building, and today it is called the Overlook.

**Right: Plate 98A. Chapman's Patent for a "Bread Cutter," 10 July 1883** (U.S. Patent Office). On 10 July 1883 Nathan Chapman was granted Patent No. 280,796 in Washington for a bread cutter. It consisted of a board with uprights to hold the loaf and guide the knife in cutting slices of uniform thickness. Undoubtedly the apparatus was used to good advantage in the kitchen of the Veranda House.

# Siasconset and Surfside

**Plate 99. The Steam Road Roller, after 1894** (Nantucket Historical Association Collection). The road from Nantucket Town to Siasconset was notoriously bad—it was popularly described as a dozen set of wheel ruts through the sand. In 1824 Peter F. Ewer had dignified the route by placing mile markers of stone along it, and afterward it was called the Milestone Road. When the railroad was under consideration in 1879 several critics suggested that the money could be spent to better advantage on the Siasconset carriage road: five years later some improvements were finally made.

In 1894 the road was macadamized, and on October 12th a steam road roller was brought to the island to facilitate the work. The machine was a product of the O. S. Kelly Company of Springfield. When the work was finished, the old Milestone Road became the new State Road. In the spring of 1896, by the side of the State Road, a three-foot-wide cycle path was constructed, its expense defrayed by private subscriptions. At that time there were only two well-paved roads on Nantucket, the long one to Siasconset and a short one to Brant Point.

Above: **Plate 100. Betsy Cary's Tavern, Broadway, Siasconset, late 19th c.** (Photograph by Henry S. Wyer, Nantucket Historical Association Collection). On the west side of Broadway, opposite New Street, is a house (left side of the photograph) whose earliest part is said to date from the 1680s. It originally stood on Sachacha Pond, about two miles north of the village. This was the crudest sort of house, framed with round posts. Its twelve-by-fifteen-foot main room probably had a fireplace on the earth floor (the wall behind being plastered), with an open wood stack above to carry off the smoke. Two tiny chambers, about seven by seven-and-a-half feet each, were at one end. After its removal to Siasconset the house was given wood floors, brick hearth and chimney, and "wart" extensions front and back, almost doubling the size of the chambers. Later an addition greater than the original house was added on the south end. The building was Elizabeth Cary's tavern and general store in 1860, when a writer from *Harper's* visited it while working on an article about the island. The "public reception room," he said, offered for sale: "Dried codfish, bottled beer, sugar-candy, fishing lines and hooks, eggs, whiskey, ginger-cakes, opodeldoc [a saponacious liniment combining camphor and other oils], pork, cigars, cheese, Ridgeway's Ready Relief, tobacco, ship biscuits, Pain Killer, Jack-knives, lucifer-matches, and jewelry." Betsy Cary, who almost three decades earlier had a boardinghouse on lower Main Street (eventually taken over by Elisha Starbuck; see Plate 21), now was described as a "a little old woman with a motherly vinegar aspect," whose civility appeared only at the sight of the customer's money. A sketch of her (Plate 100A) was among the article's illustrations. She is dressed in a black silk gown, white turban and apron, and is shown offering her wares.

Right: **Plate 100A. "Mother Cary"** (From *Harper's New Monthly Magazine*, 1860, Atheneum Collection).

**Plate 101. Capt. William Baxter in the Mail Wagon, Siasconset, late 1860s–early 1870s** (Stereograph by Josiah Freeman, Nantucket Historical Association Collection). William Baxter, a former mariner, became Betsy Cary's son-in-law and resided in her house. Besides driving the coach between Nantucket and Siasconset, Capt. Baxter brought the mail. As he came over the hill on Main Street he would blow his tin "fish" horn, as they are known on the island, to alert the inhabitants. They would assemble at the corner of Broadway and New Street, and Baxter collected a penny for each letter or paper delivered. In this posed picture the ancient mariner demonstrates his bugle technique to an unresponsive audience. Betsy Carey's tavern (behind the mail wagon) acquired the quarterboard from a ship wrecked in 1852 at Tom Nevers Head. The tavern then took the ship's name, "Shanunga," as its own.

**Plate 102. Frederick C. Sanford House, Siasconset, late 1860s** (Stereograph by Josiah Freeman, Nantucket Historical Association Collection). Frederick C. Sanford owned the great white clapboard residence at the southeast corner of Federal and Broad Streets in Nantucket, and in 1857 he paid Edward G. Kelly $600 for a little shingled cottage in Siasconset. Described as being bounded on the north, east and south sides by roads, it stood at the intersection of what were later called Main Street and Broadway, with Elbow Lane at its back. The house is said to have occupied the site as early as 1814, and had been the home of Peter Myrick, James Macy and Daniel Jones. As Sanford had done in town, he later (1863) purchased an adjoining strip for a garden on the west side of the Siasconset cottage. This piece of land had for-

merly belonged to Philip H. Folger. The cottage itself had been given an end chimney and lean-to addition around mid-century, perhaps for Sanford. The gable window here lacks sashes, which may have been removed in summer to cool the upper chamber from the sun's rays on the low roof. Freeman's picture was made during the late 1860s, and he has included a priceless collection of costumed characters, ranging from the portly gentleman in white top hat and frock coat (before the front door) to the older woman in a black hoop skirt and child with bonnet and pantalets (right). Sanford's Siasconset cottage had disappeared by the mid-1880s, and his house in town was razed during the early 1960s to make way for the present Town Building.

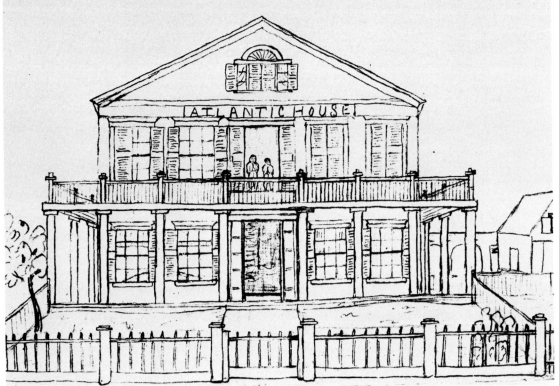

Opposite, top: **Plate 103. The Atlantic House, Main Street, Siasconset, late 19th c.** (Photograph by Henry S. Wyer, Nantucket Historical Association Collection). The oldest extant building on the island constructed specifically as a hotel, the Atlantic House on Main Street in Siasconset was opened by Henry S. Crocker in 1848. The clapboarded Greek Revival building was surrounded at first-story level by a square-piered porch, with railing and an open deck above. A transverse hallway bisecting the building gave access to square rooms on either side. The third story was lighted by a Palladian window in the pediment and skylights along the sloping roof. Atlantic House patrons came from town by stagecoach, the original attraction being the salubrious air at the east end of the island. The pleasures of surf bathing were discovered later, but were, unfortunately, at an inconvenient distance from the hotel. The first theatrical and musical evenings at Siasconset were presented here, forecasting the village's role as a thespian vacation center after the turn of the century. The Atlantic House continued as a hostelry until about World War I. Afterward the building was cut down, shifted sideways on the lot and is now used as a private summer home.

Opposite, bottom: **Plate 103A. Drawing of the Atlantic House by a Youthful Early Visitor, Annie D. Swift of Achushnet, Mass., late 19th c.** (Nantucket Historical Association Collection).

Above: **Plate 104. Footbridge at Siasconset, ca. 1873** (Stereograph by Josiah Freeman, Nantucket Historical Association Collection). Charles H. Robinson and Dr. Franklin A. Ellis purchased considerable land in partnership on Sunset Heights in 1872. One area was reserved for an Inn (Plate 106), and the balance was divided for sale as private lots. Robinson built cottages on some of them; others were sold without structures. In Freeman's view can be seen the first of Robinson's vacation houses. It is a plain building of moderate size, with a veranda enveloping the lower story. Later examples became more elaborate. The summer colony on Sunset Heights was provided with a footbridge (shown here) to the main section of Siasconset Village, spanning South Gulley, which cuts down to Codfish Park and the beach. With no obstacles eastward to the ocean, the view from the footbridge was and is superb.

The building to the right is on a separate piece of property, perhaps serving as a stable or other outbuilding for the adjoining Ocean View House (Plate 106).

Above: **Plate 105. Footbridge at Siasconset, Another View, late 19th c.** (David Gray Collection). This glimpse of the 'Sconset overpass, taken perhaps twenty years later than Plate 104, shows that the footbridge has become a popular rendezvous. The view it provides is still a primary attraction, as evidenced by the varied group of people enjoying the sights. Beyond the self-consciously posed woman at the left is the east flank of the Ocean View House.

Opposite, top: **Plate 106. The Ocean View House, Siasconset, late 1870s** (Stereograph by Josiah Freeman, Nantucket Historical Association Collection). The first building erected in Siasconset specifically as a hotel after the Atlantic House (Plate 103) was the Ocean View House. Situated at the east end of Main Street at the beginning of Sunset Heights, it took its name from the water prospect. Constructed by its owner, the builder Charles H. Robinson, the little Victorian Gothic building of vertical boards (left) contained a fruit and candy store, parlor and dining room downstairs, and seven lodging rooms above. It was opened in June 1873 under the management of Peleg Thurston. The proprietor netted a better first season than the owner, as Thurston "stuck" his "confiding friends to a considerable amount, and [skipping town] left them to whistle for their just dues" (reported the *Inquirer and Mirror*). Robinson built a new pavilion (right) that was ready for occupancy in 1876. It was shingled and in the bracketed style and stood in front of the original building, to which it was connected by a porch and pergola. The old parlor was incorporated into the dining room, and the later pavilion (still standing) accommodated the new parlor, as well as many additional guest rooms. Standing by the fancy arched gateway announcing the location, "Sunset Heights," is the three-seater depot wagon that conveyed guests between Straight Wharf and the Ocean View House.

Opposite, bottom: **Plate 107. Advertisement for Underhill's Seaside Cottages** (From the *Inquirer and Mirror*, 21 May 1898, Atheneum Collection). Vacation houses began to germinate in Siasconset along Main Street following the opening of the Atlantic House at mid-century (Plate 103), and their construction accelerated along the crest overlooking the ocean after Robinson began the development of Sunset Heights (Plate 104). Other promoters entered the game, and the result was a seasonal colony. The phenomenon was memorialized in A. Judd Northrop's book *'Sconset Summer Life*, published in 1881. Soon afterward, Edward F. Underhill, a yearly visitor from New York, joined the ranks of real-estate dealers, first selling lots, then buying, remodeling, building and renting cottages. He also delved into the history and traditions of Siasconset and wrote about them with charm and sentiment. Underhill coined the sobriquet "Patchwork Village," which was used in the titles of several of his publications, including *A Picture Book of ye Patchwork Village, 'Sconset by ye Sea* (1885) and *The Credible Chronicles of the Patchwork Village* (1886). By 1890 he had thirty-six cottages, which could be engaged by contacting his New York office. Later in the decade his advertisements, like the one shown here, were illustrated with sketches of his offerings and scenes in Siasconset, convincing the skeptic of the village's picturesqueness and amenities.

## FURNISHED SEASIDE COTTAGES,
### AT SIASCONSET, NANTUCKET.

AN ANCIENT 'SCONSET COTTAGE.

Fifty miles out in the ocean, one can have all the benefits and none of the discomforts of a sea voyage.

Life is undisturbed by the clank of machinery, the creak of ship's timbers or the roll of the vessel.

No fear of drifting on land in darkness or in fog, or being driven on a lee shore in gales.

Cool and quiet by night and by day 'SCONSET is a haven of rest for brain workers and tired out business men, and is a natural sanitarium for those suffering from nervous exhaustion, hay fever or malaria.
It is a paradise for children.

Laziness drifts into sleep and sleep awakens into laziness ; so gradual is the change, it is hard to tell where one ends and the other begins.

The most restful climate for invalids and convalescents.

Influenced by the tonic properties of the ocean air extinct appetites are born again and manifest agressive activity. It is not unusual for an invalid to gain 25 to 40 pounds during a season.

**UNDERHILL.**

'SCONSET BEACH DORIES.

NANTUCKET is the island of long lives. More than half of its people live to from 70 to 100 years. The average duration of life is 64 years, nearly double that in any other part of the world. 'SCONSET is its most wholesome spot.

AN ANCIENT 'SCONSET COTTAGE.

Life is passed basking in the sun, on the grass, or on the beach, resting in hammocks or under awnings, riding or sauntering over moors redolent with a perfume of wild flowers, fishing, or playing the current outdoor games, viewing the gorgeous sunsets or the ocean in sunshine or in storm, laving in surf of a uniform temperature of 70 degrees in July and August, while the average highest of the air is from 68 to 70.

Picturesque cottages with six to nine rooms fully furnished are to let there at from $90 to $175 for the season.

If you want to know anything more about 'SCONSET write for a circular, containing a brief history of the place with maps, views and ground plans of the houses.

♦ ♦ ♦ ♦

108 Fulton Street, New York.

Opposite, top: **Plate 108. The Beach at Siasconset, First View, late 19th c.** (Photograph by Henry S. Wyer, Anonymous Private Collection). The 20 July 1872 issue of the *New York Tribune* had sympathetic words about children spending the summer at Siasconset: "Poor little things! There is no amusement for them . . . but paddling in the sand." The children shown here are not even amusing themselves in the sand; they are lounging around a drag or barrel cart, which, when in use, was hitched behind a horse. The children's costume and demeanor seem to indicate they are natives of the old fishing village. The scene is just north of Middle Gulley, the original main access to the community from the shore. The barn on the left has a primitive clapboard roof on purlins (one can be seen through the hole), the forerunner to the shingled roof not only here but throughout the eastern part of North America. Houses on the rise are on Front Street of Siasconset.

Opposite, bottom: **Plate 109. The Beach at Siasconset, Second View, late 19th c.** (Photograph by Henry S. Wyer, Nantucket Historical Association Collection). Women's bathing attire at the beginning of the second half of the nineteenth century had been the bloomer costume of red flannel with the hair protected by a cap of oiled silk. By the last quarter of the century beachwear was of cotton or wool, and the bloomer undergarment

had been exchanged for stockings—bolder female bathers exposed the legs from the knees down. The boy's striped suit in the right foreground looks like jersey and is a forecast of the dominant type well into the twentieth century. The Ocean View House (Plate 106) introduced bathing rooms to the Siasconset beach in 1875, thus officially launching the long-awaited facilities. A dip in the brine from ankle to waist was considered by most visitors to be adequate for reaping the benefits and joys of the seashore. A few daring souls actually swam.

Above: **Plate 110. The Beach at Siasconset, Third View, late 19th c.** (Photograph by Henry S. Wyer, Nantucket Historical Association Collection). Well back from the surf and shunning sea water and sun alike, most of the summer colony at Siasconset during the 1880s lounged on the beach fully clothed; some wore gloves, and not a single head was bare. Some have stretched squares of canvas over the horizontal poles, and tied up the ends with cords, though the overcast sky hardly warrants protection from the sun. On a bright day the tent line was practically continuous. The upright frames constituted permanent beach fixtures throughout the summer. The off-islanders' frequenting of the beach differed from that of the natives mostly in being a planned and deliberate process. It was an escape from the workaday routine.

Opposite, top: **Plate 111. The *Dionis* and Carriages at Surfside, 1881** (Photograph by Henry S. Wyer, Richard P. Swain Collection). Philip H. Folger, grandson and namesake of the earlier Nantucket entrepreneur (Plates 3, 46 and 66), was involved in various "cottage-city" projects around the island. On 11 August 1879, in a new endeavor, Folger brought over a team of engineers to survey for a railroad. It was intended to serve the Cliff area, north of the town, swing over to Long Pond, at the west end, and run along the south shore through Surfside to Siasconset. The following year grading was begun, but the route ran from town straight down to Surfside and got only halfway to Siasconset. In 1881 tracks were laid over the three miles to the south shore, and on July 4th, for the first time, a train ran on Nantucket. The equipment was all secondhand and narrow-gauge (thirty-six inches). The engine had been made by the Baldwin works at Philadelphia, and had served on the Danville, Olney and Ohio River Railroad in Illinois before it was purchased at a bargain price. It was called *Dionis*—the name emblazoned in gold letters on both sides of the tender—after the wife of Tristram Coffin, patriarch of the island. There were two passenger cars, of open, summer style, which had been "broken in" on the Long Island Railroad. They could carry one-hundred-and-eighty closely-packed passengers. Glass windows were at the ends to keep cinders out of passengers' eyes, and roll-down curtains were provided on the sides, in readiness for inclement weather. The train is shown here by the platform at Surfside, with engineer Clarence M. Stansbury at the controls.

Opposite, bottom: **Plate 112. The Surfside Depot, 1881** (David Gray Collection). At the time trains began running in 1881 the dream of Surfside as a booming island resort was far from realized. A short distance away to the west were the lifesaving station (Plate 11) and several shacks, but as yet there was nothing at Surfside proper, and the railroad company found it expedient to build. The result was a plain batten-board structure, set back about fifty feet from the tracks on the ocean front, with a shallow porch along the side toward the train. The low and narrow platform by the rails (seen also at the left of Plate 111) kept passengers from having to alight in the sand. The depot served at various times as ticket office, lounge, bathing pavilion, restaurant,

ballroom and skating rink. It was three weeks from completion when the train brought the first crowds out on July 4th, but with red, white and blue decorations the building provided a festive setting for the noon clambake, followed by appropriate speeches and songs from the glee club. While the celebrations were taking place a coupling broke on the train back in town, but the engineer ran the locomotive out to relay the news that repairs were progressing. Then he returned with the cars. Since other landmarks for identifying the locale were scarce, the name "Surf Side" was lettered on the roof of the depot.

Above: **Plate 113. The Coffin Family Reunion, Surfside, August 1881** (Photograph by George H. Gardner, Nantucket Historical Association Collection). After the opening of the railroad the second important event on Nantucket during the summer of 1881 was the Coffin family reunion: the Clan Coffin Celebration. The train provided transportation to Surfside, where the principal collations were held. Accompanying the reunion were two publications on the family's island founder: Allen Coffin's succinct *Life of Tristram Coffin,* and Mrs. Harriet B. Worron's expansive *"Trustum" and His Grandchildren, by One of Them.* On the first day of the meetings the train carted about five hundred members of the Coffin family out to Surfside during the noon hour. At one-thirty George H. Gardner of Boston assembled them on the bank for a group picture. The small fry sat on the ground in front, the venerable generation in chairs behind, and the ablebodied ranged themselves in a standing mass. At the last minute Hill's New Bedford Brass Band arrived by rail, and band members in plumed shakos and shoulder straps took places at the rear. After the photographing, the clan repaired to the station to partake of a varied shore meal. Allen Coffin, secretary of the association, extended welcome, and Tristram Coffin of Poughkeepsie spoke on the early history of the family and, in particular, about his namesake. Poems and band music followed. On the third and last day of the reunion, Surfside was again the scene of a three-o'clock banquet. A ball was scheduled at the depot afterward, but the weather got boisterous, and the Coffins traveled back to town, where the final celebration was held at Atlantic Hall on Main Street instead.

THE NEW SURF-SIDE HOTEL.

Above: **Plate 114. The Surfside Hotel, Partly Collapsed, December 1899.** (Nantucket Historical Association Collection). The Surfside Land Company did its best to dispose of cottage lots and create a summer colony, and in 1882 it opened a realty office in the Surfside depot. The claim was made that three hundred lots were sold; but nobody built a house. The land company decided to prime the pump by erecting a hotel. Following the precedent set by the railroad, the new facility was a secondhand import from the mainland. It had been the Riverside Hotel on the Providence River. The design was by Walker & Company of Providence, but the original grandiose scheme with long wings had been curtailed to a central pavilion without proposed superstructure and roof terrace. Still it was a substantial building of five levels with a piazza across the front of the first floor. The building was taken apart and brought to the island, where it was reassembled (a bit differently) during the spring of 1883. It housed a billiard room and storage spaces in the basement, a large dining hall and parlor, a lobby and four reception or supper rooms on the main floor, and, on each of the upper three floors, eighteen guest rooms and facilities off the hall. The kitchen and employees' quarters were in a separate pavilion. The Surfside Hotel was situated near Nobadeer Pond, and the railroad had to be lengthened a mile. Functions formerly staged at the Surfside depot henceforth were held at the hotel. After the railroad stopped running to the south in 1895 the Surfside Hotel was abandoned and became dilapidated. It was blown down in two stages by storms at the end of the century.

Left: **Plate 114A. The Surfside Hotel** (From the *Inquirer and Mirror*, 16 June 1883, Atheneum Collection).

# Transportation

Above: **Plate 115. The *'Sconset* and Closed Passenger Car at the Siasconset Station, 1885** (David Gray Collection). In 1884 the Nantucket Railroad was further developed, when its tracks were lengthened six miles beyond the Surfside Hotel to Siasconset, the original proposed destination. The new stretch passed Madequecham, Toupchue and Forked Ponds, Tom Nevers Head and Low Beach, and it provided passengers a spectacular ride along the ocean front. But the extension was a headache to the company, as winter storms made frequent repairs and annual replacements necessities. As the recent Surfside Hotel had taken over most of the duties of the Surfside depot, the latter was divided and half of it brought and set up at Siasconset. A second train was provided in 1885. It was pulled by a little bogie engine, built by the Mason Locomotive Works of Taunton. The engine had served several years on the Boston, Revere Beach and Lynn Railroad and was on lease to the island system. Christened the *'Sconset,* its name appeared on the sides of the fuel compartment. It pulled the first piece of new rolling stock purchased by the Nantucket Railroad. Constructed by the J. C. Brill Company of Philadelphia, the car had open platforms at the ends and eight compartments to either side of a center aisle, accommodating sixty-four passengers. There was also a baggage car, a former flatcar that had been boxed in for the purpose, and which, when provided with wooden benches, could also carry passengers. The three vehicles constituted the excursion train, taking groups to grand illuminations and July 4th fireworks, clambakes, theatricals and beach parties at Siasconset.

The Nantucket Railroad ran for the last time in 1917; the following year it was sold for scrap iron. The only survivor on the island is the Brill coach, lacking wheels, which is at the Straight Wharf Crossing, servicing as the cozy bar of the Club Car Restaurant (Plate 115A).

Below: **Plate 115A. The Club Car Bar, Straight Wharf.**

**Plate 116. Steamboat Wharf, ca. 1890** (Nantucket Historical Association Collection). The wharf at the end of Broad Street changed considerably over the twenty years since Freeman made the northeast view from South Tower about 1870 (Plate 38). Buildings of the earlier era have disappeared, and in their place are the railroad depot (foreground) built in 1884, with Adams' boat shop adjoining. Beyond is the catboat basin (a white catboat can be seen in the center of the photograph). To the left of the walkway is the Old Colony Restaurant, operated by Calvert Handy before he transferred to the Central House (Plate 88). To the right at the end of Steamboat Wharf is the freight house. The boat landing was then on the south (right) side. In this view the *Island Home* has left her berth and is headed for the jetties' channel around Brant Point. The pre-1901 lighthouse stands far back from the point itself and is not visible here. Those who have just bid farewell to departing friends and relatives stop for refreshment at the Old Colony or wend their way homeward.

Top: **Plate 117. Horse-drawn Barge and "Bobtailed" Rail Cars at North Beach Street and Brant Point Road, early 1890s** (From a copper halftone plate, *Inquirer and Mirror,* 27 June 1921, Atheneum Collection). In the spring of 1881 Nantucket considered establishing horse railways, running from town to the Cliff Shore bathing beach and to Siasconset. The steam line was building its tracks southward and became a reality; the horsecar proposals failed to develop. But at the end of the decade another horse system was considered, this time with an electric line as well. Both operations sought permission to grade and lay tracks from the selectmen. Finally, in 1890 the horse line succeeded: the Beach Street Railway Company was given the right to install rails from the corner of Federal and Pearl Streets. Later the starting point of the tracks was pushed back to Main Street and its end point was extended along Brant Point Road to the lighthouse. Altogether the route was less than a dozen blocks. Vehicles consisted of two "bobtailed" or single-horse coaches. From Brant Point Road patrons had a free transfer to an omnibus or horse-drawn barge (seen in the foreground), that continued the ride to the bathing beach (Plate 123), or a short walk to the Nantucket Hotel (extreme left) from the end of the line. Thomas G. Macy, head of the company, anticipated a second line to Siasconset, but the expansion scheme fizzled in 1893. Macy and his associates later took over the steam line for two years and introduced gasoline conveyances. The horsecars to Brant Point were dragged along through the summer of 1894. Their tracks remained a nuisance in Nantucket streets another four years, when they were finally removed, and with them disappeared the last vestiges of rail cars in town. The photograph was taken from the tower of the Point Breeze Hotel (Plate 122).
Bottom: **Plate 117A. Sketch of "Bobtailed" Rail Car.**

# The Great Hotels

**Plate 118. The Nantucket, Brant Point, mid-1880s** (Photograph by Henry S. Wyer, Nantucket Historical Association Collection). In the winter of 1883 two buildings were moved from town out to Brant Point. The first was the old Friends meetinghouse on Main Street at Ray's Court (1831), later a straw-hat factory, then Atlantic Hall and eventually a skating rink (Plate 42); the second was a dwelling on Orange Street. The meetinghouse became the center pavilion, the residence the east end, and an existing summerhouse the west end of a transient hotel. The elements were all connected by four-storied wings, but the effect was better from a distance than up close. Two gazebos, of different contours, and a variety of dormer-window shapes on top, plus several balconies hung on the walls added more shadows than substance to the building design. The hostelry was conceived and sponsored by a Boston architect, George F. Hammond, who had purchased several cottage lots along the beach front facing the new jetties for its site. A shallow porch ran along the two-hundred-foot front at beach level, and the title of the hotel figured in six-foot letters. Originally to have been called The Driftwood, before opening in the summer of 1884 the name was fixed as The Nantucket. In plain view to passengers on the steamers rounding Brant Point, the building, of unprecedented size on the island, was for a while its leading hotel. Before the opening of the 1886 season the east wing (the Orange Street import) was shifted to the rear and a larger, three-storied addition was built to replace it.

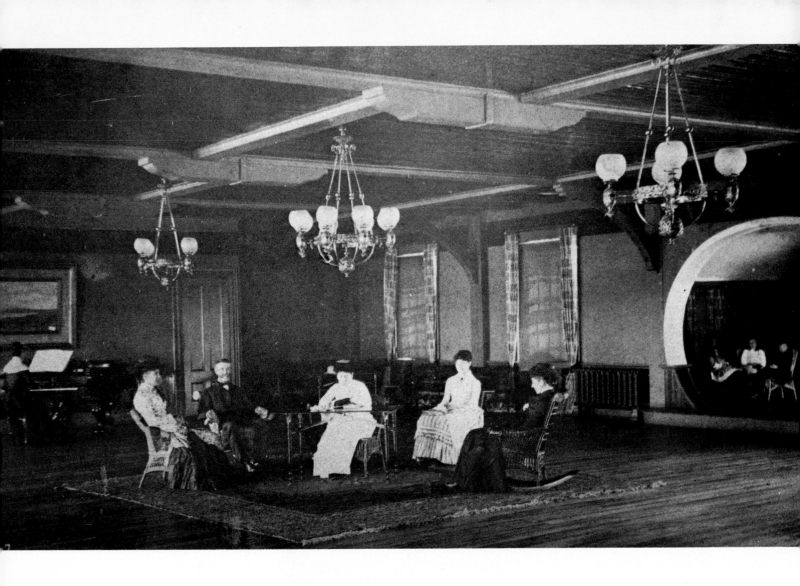

Above: **Plate 119. The Grand Parlor, The Nantucket, late 19th c.** (Photograph by Platt Bros., Nantucket Historical Association Collection). The interior of The Nantucket was as casual as the exterior. The central (meetinghouse) pavilion housed the forty-five-by-sixty-four-foot dining hall at ground level, and was furnished with imitation mahogany table and chairs. Also below were the office, barbershop, baggage room and "gent's toilet." In an ell were the kitchen, with space for the boiler, the latter supplying steam for cooking as well as for heating the dining hall and parlor. The grand parlor was immediately above the dining hall. Its ceiling was supported by trusses, to eliminate post supports. Walls were papered, floors polished, and windows hung with shades and portieres. Furniture was mostly wicker. A door led to the deck in front, and a circular opening at the back framed an elevated alcove described in the *Inquirer and Mirror* as "utilized for the presentation of parlor theatricals, or for the use of the orchestra when it may be desired." Stairways were to either side of the parlor and dining room, and corridors beyond led to one hundred chambers in the wings. Electric bells in guest rooms connected with the office, where J. S. Doyle, a former manager of the Ocean House, presided. A detached building at the rear of the hotel contained a "billiard and bowling salon and bar," and the employees' quarters. Before the first summer season of 1884 was ended, a bathhouse was added. The Nantucket's last full season was in 1904. Its contents were auctioned off in 1905, and at the beginning of 1906 the central pavilion was brought back to town, sited on south Water Street, and became the Red Man's Hall and Dreamland Theatre. The rest of the building was taken apart and converted to seaside cottages along Hulbert Avenue. Its transient days were over.

Opposite, top: **Plate 120. The Sea Cliff Inn, Cliff Road, late 1880s** (Photograph by Henry C. Platt, Nantucket Historical Association Collection). Nantucket's leading hotel for more than fourscore years, the Sea Cliff Inn was a dominant factor in affecting the change of the name of North Street to the present Cliff Road. Its elevated site provided a broad panorama of Nantucket Sound and the Great Harbor, with glimpses of Great Point light and the eastern headlands of the island. The original pavilion of the Sea Cliff Inn was designed by Robert A. Slade, framed in Maine and erected by the local builder Charles H. Robinson, owner of the Ocean View House (Plate 106). The Sea Cliff Inn was commissioned and operated by Mrs. Charlotte W. Pettee, an established boardinghouse mistress here, who opened her hostelry in 1887. The building was the first Nantucket hotel in the "Queen Anne" style, with both clapboards and shingles on the walls, a variety of dormer types on the complex roof, elaborate crestings and tall chimney shafts. The little semidetached pavilion at the far end was an early-nineteenth-century dwelling, to which had been added hoods over the door and windows, and a gambrel gable on the third story, to tie it in with the new structure. This building served as the kitchen and lodging for domestics. The main story of the hotel itself included the dining room, with a piazza and parlor at the front, and a stairhall and office in the center. Mrs. Pettee's quarters were behind the desk (Plate 120A). There were some forty guest rooms.

Opposite, bottom: **Plate 120A. The Reception Hall, the Sea Cliff Inn, late 19th c.** (Photograph by H. C. Platt, Nantucket Historical Association Collection).

**Plate 121. The Enlarged Sea Cliff Inn, late 19th c.**
(Photograph by Henry S. Wyer, Nantucket Historical Association
Collection). A new building (right of center) was constructed in
1893 and connected by a twenty-five-foot "midway" to the north
end of the original Sea Cliff Inn (left of center). The work was
directed by E. T. Carpenter of Foxboro, and the addition was
considerably larger than the parent building. It had a higher basement and was four full stories in front with a porch spanning the
facade. Ascending from the foyer was an imperial staircase, with a
huge parlor at the south end and several reception rooms to the
north. In the basement was a billiard room (under the great
parlor) and an assembly hall with a stage and seating capacity for
three hundred (under the rear wing). Above were seventy-five
guest rooms. At the summit of the stair tower terminating the wing
was a sun parlor opening to the flat sun deck. Guests could pass
under the "midway" to a path descending the bank and connecting with a plank walk (foreground) that led to the water for bathing, boating or fishing. At the completion of the new building the
entire complex was equipped with electricity. The Sea Cliff Inn's
last season was the summer of 1972, and after that it was razed. In
the spring of 1977 the lower cliff region was spoiled by the building
of nine tennis courts with chain-link fences around them and accompanying structures.

**Plate 122. The Point Breeze Hotel, Easton Street, late 19th c.** (From John F. Murphy, *Sixty-five Views of Nantucket*, n. d., Atheneum Collection). In the fall of 1888 the Elijah H. Alley home and adjoining lots on the north side of Easton Street, opposite the Springfield Annex No. 1, were purchased by Charles F. Folger of Philadelphia. His intention was said to be the erection of a first-class restaurant. But a hotel was built instead during the winter and spring of 1890–91 by Edwin R. Smith, carpenter, and John C. Ring, mason. The building had three full floors above a high basement, with a square turret on the southeast corner one story taller, and garret rooms under the roof. A plain porch at the main level spanned the sixty-two-foot front. In the basement were the billiard and bowling rooms, toilets, porter's room and storerooms. On the first floor were the office, parlor, two dining rooms

and two sleeping apartments. The kitchen was in a separate pavilion. The principal building contained a total of forty rooms, and the Alley-house annex provided ten more. The hotel was a bit inland, on a site even with the base of Brant Point but received breezes from that headland, and some of the rooms provided water views. Up-to-date conveniences included an electric signal system, which was operated by its own generating plant, and telephones, such as had been installed recently in the nearby Springfield House. The tangle of electric wires, suspended from poles along the street, soon provided electric lights as well. This building was destroyed by fire in 1925, but an adjoining pavilion of great size had been built in 1903–4 and stands today as the Gordon Folger Hotel.

**Plate 123. Cliff Shore Bathing Beach, late 19th c.**
(Photograph by Henry S. Wyer, Nantucket Historical Association
Collection). In 1848 the Ocean House advertised "good accommodations for Sea Bathing," but what these were is not stated. In the
spring of 1864 the proprietor, Eben Allen, announced that there had
been "erected a Bathing House on the Shore, where persons can
enjoy Sea-Bathing." This was probably a building with individual
cubicles in which people could change into beach attire. The bathing house was "open on pleasant days between the hours of 10 and 1
o'clock in the forenoon, and from 4 to 7 afternoons." Tickets were
fifteen cents, with packages of ten tickets costing one dollar. The
Cliff Shore suffered somewhat from the establishing of Charles E.
Hayden's Clean Shore Bathing Rooms on the cove between Steamboat Wharf and Brant Point in 1869, as the latter was more convenient to existing hostelries. In 1880 Hayden also began operating
bathhouses under the cliff at the west end of Beachside. The transportation problem was solved by running the sloop *Dauntless* from
Old North Wharf every two hours; the fee was ten cents each way.
With the building of the Sea Cliff Inn in 1887 the Cliff Shore Bathhouses were assured steady patronage. Several cottages of the late
1880s on Sherburne Heights break the skyline (right) in this
photograph.

# Recreation Centers

**Plate 124. The Race Tack at the Fairgrounds, early 20th c.** (From a postcard, Paul Madden Collection). In 1856 the attempt had been made to prove that the island was no longer, as the *Nantucket Inquirer* put it, "only a barren sand heap" but had "many fine and profitable farms," whose tenants found "a ready market . . . here at their very door." The Nantucket Agricultural Society was formed, and on October 28th both professional farmers and amateur gardeners were given an exhibition of their products in Atheneum Hall. When the exhibition was repeated the following year, a stock show was added, and ploughing and spading matches were held in the lot behind. In 1859 the Society acquired ten acres for permanent fairgrounds in South Pasture, below the first milestone on the Siasconset Road. The land was "handsomely fenced, and suitable buildings, stands, & c. [were] erected." Vegeta-

ble displays, joined by arts and crafts, continued to be held in the upper hall of the Atheneum, at least until 1885, when they were moved to the skating rink in Atlantic Hall on Main Street. Conservative Nantucket took pride in its achievements in horticulture and animal husbandry; and as late as 1868 the write-up on the fair emphasized that these activities were quite enough, adding, although there was a horse show "We are grateful it has not been *horse racing.*" But in 1872 the horse show was followed by a trotting race, and it became an annual event. The judge's stand was built by Charles H. Robinson in 1879. The grandstand was small and must have been built in 1894, for in the September 5th–6th fair of that year a ten-cent fee for a seat in the structure was added for the first time to the twenty-cent entrance charge.

Opposite, top: **Plate 125. The Wauwinet House, ca. 1876** (Stereograph by Josiah Freeman, Nantucket Historical Association Collection). The popularity of resorts (present about the Great Harbor since the late eighteenth century) increased in the late 1860s with the revival of the "squantum." This was a cruise to a remote location with a party at the destination. In 1876 Charles A. Kenney and Asa W. N. Small contributed to the cult by establishing the Wauwinet House at the Head of the Harbor, below the Haulover, a narrow neck of land connecting Coatue and Great Point to the main part of the island. The site had the advantage of providing both harbor and ocean beaches. Named after the Indian tribe that had once lived here, the Wauwinet House was a building about thirty-feet square. The entire first story was occupied by an entertainment room, with walls on hinges so they could be opened to the breezes; the half-story above contained several chambers. A porch spanning the front looked out over the harbor and, in the distance, the town. A pier protruded into the water. The inaugural event was an invitational affair extended to the Masons, Odd Fellows and Daughters of Rebekah. The party of about one hundred and sixty came out by nine "yachts" that left Steamboat Wharf at seven o'clock in the morning of 14 June 1876. They were treated to a noon meal consisting of "clam chowder, boiled lobster and all sorts of pastry." Prof. L. H. Johnson provided music during the repast, and also for the quadrilles, polkas and waltzes that followed. Group singing and croquet occupied the afternoon until

the five-o'clock return to town. Regular passenger service to the Wauwinet House was provided by the little steamer *Island Belle* (Plate 125A), made in Capt. Codd's backyard on Orange Street. Later trips were made by the yacht *Lillian* and the launch *Siren*.

Opposite, bottom: **Plate 125A. The *Island Belle,* late 19th c.** (Stereograph by Josiah Freeman, Nantucket Historical Association Collection).

Above: **Plate 126. The Cedar Beach House, Coatue, 31 August 1886** (Photograph by Josiah Freeman, Nantucket Historical Association Collection). The Cedar Beach House was a building similar to that of the nearby Wauwinet House, and it was sponsored by one of the latter's original proprietors, Asa W. N. Small. When opened in 1883 the Cedar Beach House adjoined a two-hundred-and-seventy-five-lot development of the Coatue Land Company, and the Head of the Harbor was provided with passenger service from Town by the steam yacht *Coskata*. The entire project changed hands in 1890. The *Inquirer and Mirror* reported that under the later manager, C. F. Howard, Coatue provided "quite a large bathing establishment . . . with a toboggan slide, swings and other features . . . where hundreds of children enjoyed the exhilarating sport of a rapid shoot through the stratosphere, terminated by a plunge into the Atlantic." The Cedar Beach House had been abandoned several years before it burned to the ground in August 1908.

**Plate 127. Chadwick's Folly, Squam Head, late 19th c.**
(Marshall Ferrier Collection). Squam Head, on the east coast of
the island, between Wauwinet and Sachacha Pond, was the scene
of mysterious building activities during the early 1880s. Bricks
were being reused from the old Citizens Bank building (recently
demolished at the east corner of Main and Washington Streets in
Town) but most of the construction was of wood. A large, two-storied barn or stable was completed first (right), and work was
progressing on a larger residence-type building (left of center). It
had the severe form of a New England house, with pilasters at the
corners, clapboards on the lower walls and shingles above. The
ends of the structure were gabled, the deep eaves were bracketed,
and the roof was crowned by a large square cupola, through which
rose a central chimney. Bay windows complicated the flanks, and
a high platform encircled the building. The name of William H.

Chadwick, cashier at the Pacific National Bank, was linked with
the enterprise. Chadwick was thought to be acting as agent for
"parties abroad"; and the worst rumors had the building destined
for use as a gambling casino, with wharves below for tying up
millionaires' yachts. The volcano finally erupted when the full
story appeared in the 17 January 1885 issue of the *Inquirer and
Mirror*. The cashier had taken "between $10,000 and $15,000"
from the bank and tampered with accounts, and he had borrowed
the balance of about $50,000 privately. Chadwick's father paid off
the bank's deficit in cash; the other debts had various outcomes.
Chadwick lost his job and was sentenced to five years in jail. The
complex at Squam Head was auctioned off in 1894. Known as
"Chadwick's Folly," the buildings spent most of their existence
neglected and abandoned. In 1956 the main house and part of the
barn were razed.

# Interesting People and Events at the End of the Century

Above, left: **Plate 128. William D. Clark, Town Crier** (From Henry S. Wyer, *Nantucket in Pictures and Verse*, Nantucket, 1892, Atheneum Collection). "I'm the man who drove the first and last spike on the Nantucket Railroad and set the first telegraph pole!" shouted Billy Clark, attempting to polish his aura for the Talmadge Pilgrims, who were waiting for the train to leave for Siasconset on 5 July 1887. Three years later Billy could have added to the list his driving the first spike on the horse railway. He was the self-appointed town crier, following his "enlistment" in the Union cause during the Civil War, an episode that ended in a ninety-nine-year furlough in lieu of training. Billy's theater of operations in Nantucket ranged from fire watch in South Tower and announcements of town affairs and news along the streets, to picking up his bundle of newspapers and hawking them on the wharf. One spiel is reported (in Henry S. Wyer's *Nautucket, Picturesque and Historic*) to have run: "Now comes the news tonight! Awful fire in Chicago! City's all burnt up. Hundreds of folks drowned! That's down in Kentucky. The River Ohio's overflowin', and they can't stop it!" Another went: "Now there's a *Fearful Flood* out west—*Mississippi River's all under water!*" The tin fish horn was Billy's device for attracting attention from the tower before relaying information below about incoming ships, wrecks or other catastrophies. William D. Clark handed out engraved cards every year so his friends would not forget his birthday on November 17th. A remembrance was expected, and Billy admonished them shamelessly: "Anything but neckties!"

Above, right: **Plate 128A. Advertisement** (From the *Nantucket Journal*, 15 June 1882, Atheneum Collection).

**Plate 129. Alvin Hull, Town Crier, July 1895** (Nantucket Historical Association Collection). Billy Clark's professional rival was Alvin Hull, and for a while they were town criers together. One point of contention between them was that Hull had seen actual service in the Civil War, as a member of the Twentieth Massachusetts Regiment, at Antietam and Harper's Ferry. Since Hull was of small build and an expert rider, Col. Jeffries of the Seventh Ohio later selected him for his mounted orderly. Afterward Hull affected a soldierly swagger in uniform attire. In 1889, Capt. Anthony Smalley was up for reelection as state representative, and Hull was on the scene when the votes were counted after the election. When it seemed likely that Smalley would win, Hull dashed off to inform the candidate. But as he neared Smalley's house he had misgivings and turned back for confirmation. Catching sight of Billy Clark coming full-steam from the polling place, Hull guessed the result and sped to complete his mission. But Clark swerved into a side street, leaped several fences, and arrived at the rear of the captain's residence with just enough wind to sound a blast on his fish horn. Smalley came to the window, Clark extended his hand, speechless but smiling, as Hull began knocking on the front door. A week later Hull was circulating a petition seeking appointment as keeper of the Brant Point lighthouse.

Alvin Hull gave the July 4th oration on the Square in 1892. He was carried away by his own eloquence and seemed unperturbed by the bursting of a firecracker affixed to his shoe, or the hissing of a "fizzer" dangerously close to his head. It took the explosion of a cannon cracker, planted surreptitiously under his dry-goods box rostrum, to bring his peroration to a close.

**Plate 130. Triumphal Arch on Federal Street at Main for Nantucket's Centennial-Bicentennial Celebration, July 1895** (Nantucket Historical Association Collection). In 1895 Nantucketers commemorated the one-hundredth anniversary of the changing of the town's name from Sherburne back to Nantucket, and the two-hundredth anniversary of the incorporation of Nantucket County. Decorations were put up at Steamboat Wharf and across Main, Centre and Orange Streets at the head of the Square (Plate 129) and elsewhere. Those at the boat landing extended welcome, and others were inscribed with words appropriate to the occasion. The "triumphal arch" at Federal Street consisted of two towers connected by a lattice-truss bridge embellished with tricolored bunting and flags. Festivities began at seven o'clock in the morning of July 9th with an hour-long ringing of bells, booming of cannons and screeching of steam whistles.

Next came a band concert on the Square from eight to nine o'clock. Boat races followed in the harbor. Musical and literary exercises were held in the First Congregational Church during the remainder of the morning, continuing throughout the afternoon. Simultaneous with these activities, a band concert and baseball match between Middleton and Nantucket took place at the fairgrounds, with the island team made up entirely of summer visitors. The newspaper did not mention which side won, however. Events on July 10th were staged at Wauwinet, where fifteen hundred people were transported by boat. The noon clambake cost fifteen cents per plateful; the price included keeping the plate as a souvenir. Running and swimming matches were followed by a life-saving drill. A greased-pig contest was also scheduled, but the porker had been left on Steamboat Wharf. The two-day celebration closed with an evening band concert on lower Main Street.

**Plate 131. The Auction of the Old Windmill, August 1897**
(Photograph by Henry S. Wyer, Anonymous Private Collection).
The old windmill on Popsquatchet Hills (Plate 4) had been
purchased by John F. Sylvia for $1,200 in 1866, and thirty years
later his heirs, Lewis Francisco Cordozo and José Alexandre
Marques of the Azores Islands, ordered it to be sold at auction.
After notices appeared in the newspaper for four consecutive
weeks, the sale was held at ten o'clock in the morning of 4 August
1897. It was conducted by Charles E. Mooers in front of his auction house at the northwest corner of Main and Union Streets. The
event brought out a swarm of Nantucketers, most of them in Sun-
day dress. They ignored the sale of benches and bedsteads (to the
right of the buggy, lower left-hand corner), but took a lively
interest in the proceedings as the mill and about two-and-one-half
acres of land were sold to the Nantucket Historical Association for
$885. The mill henceforth was a museum.

On the south side of Main Street, beginning at the left, may be
seen the grooming emporium conducted by the dashing barber J.
W. Brady, who proved ill-suited to the placid mode of life on the
island. Next door is Roberts' Restaurant and Bakery, earlier
called the Washington House after the old inn that stood on its site
(Plate 44). A bicycle shop is next, and to the right of the tree trunk
may be seen a glimpse of the Post Office. On the other side of the
passway a hammock is suspended overhead between the near end
of the Central Market building and the closest elm (right of center).
Other trees serve as billboards (center, toward the rear) and poles
for utility wires. By 1977 most of the wires on lower Main Street
had been concealed, but at the beginning of summer numerous cast-
concrete benches were made permanent encroachments upon the
Square.